WRITE YOUR CONGRESSMAN

WRITE YOUR CONGRESSMAN

Constituent Communications and Representation
by Stephen E. Frantzich

PRAEGER

PRAEGER SPECIAL STUDIES • PRAEGER SCIENTIFIC

New York • Philadelphia • Eastbourne, UK
Toronto • Hong Kong • Tokyo • Sydney

Library of Congress Cataloging in Publication Data

Frantzich, Stephen E.
  Write your congressman.

  Bibliography: p.
  Includes index.
  1. United States. Congress—Constituent
communication. 2. United States. Congress—
Records and correspondence. 3. Mail preparation.
4. Political letter-writing—United States. I. Title.
JK1083.F72 1985   328.73   85-12275
ISBN 0-03-004568-1 (alk. paper)

Published in 1986 by Praeger Publishers
CBS Educational and Professional Publishing, a Division of CBS Inc.
521 Fifth Avenue, New York, NY 10175 USA

© 1986 by Praeger Publishers

6789   052   987654321

Printed in the United States of America on acid-free paper

INTERNATIONAL OFFICES

Orders from outside the United States should be sent to the appropriate
address listed below. Orders from areas not listed below should be placed
through CBS International Publishing, 383 Madison Ave., New York, NY
10175 USA

Australia, New Zealand
Holt Saunders, Pty, Ltd., 9 Waltham St., Artarmon, N.S.W. 2064, Sydney,
Australia

Canada
Holt, Rinehart & Winston of Canada, 55 Horner Ave., Toronto, Ontario,
Canada M8Z 4X6

Europe, the Middle East, & Africa
Holt Saunders, Ltd., 1 St. Anne's Road, Eastbourne, East Sussex, England
BN21 3UN

Japan
Holt Saunders, Ltd., Ichibancho Central Building, 22-1 Ichibancho, 3rd Floor,
Chiyodaku, Tokyo, Japan

Hong Kong, Southeast Asia
Holt Saunders Asia, Ltd., 10 Fl, Intercontinental Plaza, 94 Granville Road,
Tsim Sha Tsui East, Kowloon, Hong Kong

**Manuscript submissions should be sent to the Editorial Director, Praeger
Publishers, 521 Fifth Avenue, New York, NY 10175 USA**

To my wife Jane who provided both the conducive environment and
the constant support which made research and writing not only
possible, but also enjoyable

PREFACE

The nostrum "write your congressman" remains as a residue of high school civics classes for most American citizens. During my fifteen years of teaching, it has become clear that many students either embrace this strategy unthinkingly or increasingly express a cynicism based on revelations of ethical transgressions or self-serving public relations strategies of members of Congress. The purpose of this book is to realistically analyze the two-way communications patterns and strategies between members of Congress and the citizens they are expected to represent.

A better understanding of this communications interchange is important for members of Congress, who depend on it for their political survival, for citizens, who wish to satisfy their political interests, and for the political system, which requires a sense of legitimacy and adequate information on citizen desires and policy consequences.

It is my belief that the system works best when all participants in the two-way communications interchange have a realistic understanding of different strategies and have relatively equal potential for getting their messages heard. If you agree with the findings of this analysis and find them useful, tell others. If you find the results disturbing, I guess you can "write your congressman."

ACKNOWLEDGMENTS

Any significant writing incurs a number of debts. The students who too quickly embraced the utility of solving all problems by writing their congressmen as well as those who greeted such suggestions with raised eyebrows or pointed questions stimulated my interest in determining the actual role, patterns, and strategies of constituent communications. The over sixty members of Congress and their staffs who participated in interviews, particularly those who opened their files for perusal and duplication of documents, provided crucial information. Research support from the U.S. Congress, Office of Technology Assessment, and the Naval Academy Research Council provided the access and time needed for research. Donna Hurley and Gloria Perdue used their computerized detective skills to mine numerous bibliographic sources. Significant editorial help was provided by Jane Frantzich, Winifred Frantzich, and Sandra Erb. Bill Christ of Technicolor Government Services Inc. provided the original art work.

CONTENTS

LIST OF TABLES AND FIGURES

Tables

Figures

CHAPTER 1

CONSTITUENT COMMUNICATIONS:
Political Reality and
Democratic Theory

Dear Sir: Fellow on the radio says to write your Congressman so just
thought I would drop you a line. Yours truly (quoted in Davis 1961, p. 11)

Communication between an elected official and a constituent is mutually
beneficial. The dialogue helps shape many issues and may affect the
outcome of national legislation. (Cohen 1982, p. 3)

Little did the politicians of the 1780s, who drafted the U.S. Constitution and its supporting legislation, realize that their commitment to an
inexpensive public mail system and the granting of free mailing rights
to elected officials would lead the politicians of the 1980s to view consti-
uent communications as a primary part of their job. Were they to observe
a current congressional office, the founding fathers would be amazed at
both the volume and nature of communications. Coming from an era
wary about the rights and capabilities of the average citizen, the
originators of the Constitution saw communications as largely a one-way
street in which the more capable elected officials would try to raise the
awareness level of the most capable constituents and would expect little
response outside of election day. The representation of citizen interests
was to come about largely as a result of a selection process where elected
officials were "local products" whose life experiences allowed them to naturally look out for the interests of their friends and neighbors through
a process of "impersonation" (Eulau 1967, p. 66).

A number of broad historical trends began chipping away at this very
indirect view of representation as an adequate criterion for democracy.
In the philosophical realm, the late Middle Ages saw the Roman notion
of elected officials as agents serving by the consent of their constituents

combined with the Reformation concept that all individuals were equal before God. These themes influenced the founding fathers, but it took a century or more for the logical extension of these views to find universal acceptance, leading to the conclusion that everyone has the equal right to be heard and be represented in lawmaking (Eulau 1967, p. 66). Acceptance of the rights of the average citizen and the very broadening of the legal basis for citizenship (by granting the right to vote to non-property holders, women, and racial minorities) were facilitated by the enhanced capabilities of the average citizen brought on by increased education and mass communications. This gave all citizens at least the raw material for awareness and involvement.

REPRESENTATION AND RESPONSIVENESS

Modern definitions of representation grant the reality that only a small group of citizens can hold elected office and make decisions, but they also maintain that election is not a license to pursue one's personal preferences. Rather, election is a responsibility to open a two-way communication between the elected and the represented. In her classic work, Hannah Pitkin defined representation as "acting in the interests of the represented, in a manner responsive to them" (Pitkin 1967, p. 209). The concept of responsiveness adds an additional burden to the representative, who can no longer simply "re" "present" the interests of his constituents by assuming that his election means that his views are automatically theirs. He must inform them of the options, seek out their views, and pay heed to their preferences. While commitment to the philosophical goal of responsiveness in the abstract fails to translate into absolute constituent responsiveness in practice, the existence of such a widely held goal serves as a yardstick against which to evaluate short-cuts and shortcomings.

Traditionally, responsiveness was defined quite narrowly to include only the congruence between constituents' desires concerning public policy and the policy decisions of the elected official. Such assumptions make the unwarranted assertion that the only thing citizens want from government is to see their preferences on "collective benefits" (those policies affecting the general well-being of society) prevail. In reality, many citizens approach government to gain more parochial "selective benefits" (governmental aid for individuals and clearly defined groups) and want their elected officials to be responsive as access points for such aid (see Fenno 1978, p. 240).

A broader view of representational responsiveness is clearly in order. Eulau and Karps (1977, p. 513) delineate four basic types of responsiveness: policy responsiveness, service responsiveness, allocation responsiveness, and symbolic responsiveness.

Policy Responsiveness

Policy responsiveness emphasizes the traditional role of Congress as a policymaking body dealing with the broad issues of public policy. Responsiveness can follow from a number of mechanisms. Using an "electoral" model, one conceives of policy-minded voters matching carefully their preferences with the policy stands of candidates and voting accordingly. While operational in some critical cases, such a model involves a higher expectation of most voters' interests and capabilities than it is reasonable to expect on a regular basis. The "sharing" model assumes that much representation is involuntary and operates through the process of candidates recruited from a constituency naturally having empathy for its interests (Erikson 1978, pp. 526–32). While the latter model is more realistic about citizen capabilities, both models severely limit the potential for citizen impact.

> If constituency-representative policy agreement results from the sharing of policy preferences without active influence or responsiveness, the constituency retains no mechanism for assuring continued policy agreement, unless incumbents are regularly removed from office. (Stone 1980, p. 400)

True responsiveness requires that citizens be more directly involved in the decision making than simply sitting back and assuming that the "hometown boy" will automatically represent constituent wishes. Ideally, responsiveness involves citizens making demands on their legislators and attempting to instruct them on policy issues, and legislators seeking to assess the representativeness of the demands and weighing heavily those representing a broad range of constituents in their policy decisions. Realizing that legislators may hear little or nothing on many issues, a proponent of the "instructed" model would argue that lack of constituent demands reflects more a lack of information than a lack of interest and would make it incumbent on the legislator to seek out constituent views and anticipate interests creatively.

Service and Allocation Responsiveness

Service and allocation responsiveness involves individuals and groups of individuals petitioning their representative to intervene in the governmental process for parochial goals, such as straightening out alleged governmental misconduct affecting the petitioning individual or seeking out government benefits for the petitioner. Service responsiveness involves individual problems with the bureaucracy over everything from a missing Social Security check to introducing legislation allowing a specific individual to immigrate to the United States despite immigration quotas. The individualized nature of such casework places it in a quite different category from policy responsiveness on public issues.

Allocation responsiveness applies to the parochial interests of small groups of individuals, often small political units, and their desire to tap the government for grants to solve narrow problems. They request things like access to public information, help in preparing cases, and preferential treatment in allocating funds.

The expectation that legislators will take on such service functions stems from the original function of legislatures to present "bills of grievance" to monarchs on behalf of constituents (Loewenberg and Patterson 1979, p. 187). There is nothing in the Constitution explicitly requiring that members of Congress will be servants of their constituents in dealing with the bureaucracy,

> but the simple logic of the requirement that members are to be locally nominated and locally elected insures that they will serve—or else they take the electoral risks of not doing so. (Olson 1966, p. 340)

Symbolic Responsiveness

The concept of symbolic responsiveness is a bit more abstract than the other forms. The mere existence of the Congress as an institution ready and willing to be responsive builds diffuse support for the political system. In an era when government seems unapproachable due to its size and complexity, the existence of members of Congress with the patience and willingness to listen acts "as a kind of safety valve for citizens whose frustrations and anxieties might otherwise find destructive outlets" (Olson 1966, p. 337). The benefit of a Congress perceived as responsive does not depend on a citizen's experience. "Often citizens are content to know the direct lines of communication are there; never feeling the need to use them" (Meadow 1980, p. 76).

THE NECESSARY CONDITIONS FOR RESPONSIVENESS

In order for responsiveness to be a reality in a political system, there must be a mix of elected officials motivated to respond and capable citizens motivated to make demands, with an active two-way communications network between the two.

Legislator Motivation

Few behaviors in politics, or in any other realm for that matter, stem from purely idealistic or purely selfish motives. As Congressman Morris Udall (D–AZ) describes it, the value placed on being responsive and keeping in touch with one's constituents "is an amalgam of civic virtue and political necessity" (Tacheron and Udall 1970, p. 95).

Congressmen are not uncommitted to the ideal of responsiveness as a philosophical goal. They also realize that come election day, the candidate who is at least perceived as being responsive will have an electoral advantage. The conventional wisdom around Capitol Hill is that aside from redistricting and personal scandal, the only explanation for an incumbent losing office is through losing touch with his or her district. The key to keeping in touch is effective communications. For policy responsiveness, one does not have to agree with constituents on every issue, but one is wise to know their concerns and address the issue when your position fails to coincide with theirs. In regard to service and allocation responsiveness, there is little excuse for not seeking out constituent problems and going to bat for them to the best of one's ability. It is a low-cost expenditure of time and effort where success can be shouted from the rooftop and failure blamed on bureaucracy, whose reputation is already tarnished and thus seen by constituents as worthy of blame.

Constituent Motivation

The advice to "write your congressman" has become a panacea ballyhooed by lobbies, civic groups, political science professors, and the congressmen themselves. While many citizens question the performance and honesty of Congress as an institution (Parker and Davidson 1979), most believe that if they can get through to their own congressman he will seriously consider their views and pursue their interests. A recent study revealed that while only 22 percent of the population thought the Congress as an institution was doing an "excellent" or "pretty good" job, over 40 percent put their own congressman into those categories. The most common positive characteristics associated with individual congressmen in that study were "listening to constituents," "caring what you think," and "representing the district well" (U.S. Congress, House, Commission on Administrative Review 1977, pp. 816–19).

While belief in the right and utility of demanding responsiveness from congressmen is high, the expected subsequent behavior of making demands is more limited:

> For generations, the idea of expressing one's concern about public affairs to one's representatives in government has been a popular norm

in this country...far more people believe in this form of citizenship than
practice it...the practice is confined to roughly 15% of the adult population and is a regular practice for only about 3%. (Rosenau 1974, p. 209)

If making demands on members of Congress has not become a regular pattern for the bulk of citizens, this may not reflect a lack of commitment to the utility of so doing; rather, the low level of demand may indicate either general satisfaction with the course of events or perhaps
limited information on how and about what demands to make and how
to go about it.

Communications

Open and extensive communications between members of Congress
and their constituents is a necessary condition for breathing life into a
sterile concept such as responsiveness. Much of the responsibility for developing a communications dialogue falls to the congressman, who is in
a better position to know the issues, options, and possibilities than is the
individual citizen. Many of the prominent participants in the political history of the United States spoke eloquently of the need for government
in general and the Congress in particular to play an active role in educating the public:

> I know of no safe depository of the ultimate powers of the society but
> the people themselves; and if we think them not enlightened enough
> to exercise their control with a wholesome discretion, the remedy is not
> to take it from them but to inform their discretion. (Thomas Jefferson,
> quoted in Fulbright 1979, p. 721)

> A popular government, without popular information, or the means of
> acquiring it, is but a prologue to a farce, or a tragedy, or perhaps both.
> Knowledge will forever govern ignorance; and a people who mean to
> be their own governors must arm themselves with the power which
> knowledge gives. (James Madison, quoted in Mathias 1982a, p. S11332)

> This informing function of Congress should be preferred to even its
> legislative function. Unless [Congress informs] the country must remain
> in embarrassing, crippling ignorance of the very affairs which it is most
> important that it should understand and direct. (Woodrow Wilson,
> quoted in Mathias 1982a, p. S11332)

As a more contemporary congressman put it:

> I think a congressman has a duty to educate the public. You present
> both sides of an issue to your district and you try to persuade them to

the way you think is correct. I invite public participation in my decision-making process. I think I can teach my people why certain programs, such as the federal minimum wage, are right and important. Sometimes they convince me. (Cavanaugh 1981, p. 66)

Communicating with constituents has often been relegated to the "necessary evil" category by both members of the Congress and the public, since it does not fit into the idealized role of Congress as a deliberative body, spending its weeks and hours grappling with the great issues of the day. Perhaps we have been blinded by our definitions and have denigrated a worthy endeavor:

Rather than drawing the line separating the legislative from nonlegislative activities at what is essential to the deliberations of a house of Congress...it is urged that a better line would separate the business of government from the personal life and activities of members of Congress...the duty to assist people in securing the redress of their grievances against the government and to inform them by newsletters and speeches outside Congress, if faithfully executed, would be no less legislative if it is performed in part because it is expected by constituents and because it promotes reelection. (Kennedy 1980, p. 733)

Part of the problem leading to the low esteem of congressional communications with constituents is that much of what passes for communications is really "munications." The "co" in communications implies a two-way interchange. Much of the communication emanating from Congress is more for public consumption and political advantage than for enlightenment and responsiveness. In Richard Fenno's words, congressmen "advertise" more than communicate; and

Advertising is primarily one-way communication. The idea of responsiveness, on the other hand, assumes the existence of two-way communication....From the standpoint of democratic theory the greater the proportion of two-way communication, the more likely there is to be both electoral accountability and responsiveness on the part of the representative. (Fenno, 1978 p. 238)

In the early Congresses, members dealing with less educated constituents and limited communications channels resorted to circular letters designed to be passed around the constituency informing it of its representatives' actions in Washington and neither hoping for nor expecting a response (Cunningham 1978, p. 181; *American Historical Review* 1979, p. 847).

With members of Congress being able to dominate the communications interchange, they gained the upper hand of being selective in what they chose to report. Until constituents had ready access to alternative facts and interpretations, they had little to contribute to the communications nexus.

Contemporary citizens have a much wider range of information sources and more of them have the capabilities to identify their needs in ways comprehensible to Congress. Thus the modern citizen is in a much better position to force congressmen to make constituent communications the true two-way interchange that the goal of responsiveness would dictate.

Before we create another false image of the inquisitive constituent thirsting for information from his or her representative, it is important to interject some reality:

> Some of the more buoyant advocates of popular sovereignty have regarded the citizen as a kind of kibitzer who looks over the shoulder of his representative at the legislative game. Kibitzer and player may disagree as to which card should be played, but they were at least thought to share a common understanding of what the alternatives are.... Far from looking over the shoulder of their Congressmen at the legislative game, most Americans are almost totally uninformed about the legislative issues in Washington. (Miller and Stokes 1963, p. 47)

Not all communications from Congress enhance the public good and eschew a self-serving goal—but some do. Not all citizens stand ready with well-informed positions on issues they want to share and services they wish rendered—but some do. Not all members of Congress stand ready on all issues to put aside their personal biases and partisan commitments to follow a constituent's lead—but constituent communications do have a positive impact at some times.

The remainder of this book will take the philosophical grounding for effective congressional-constituent communications as a given, explore in more detail the actual pattern of the two-way congressional-constituent communications as it now exists, and speculate on some of the future trends.

CHAPTER 2

THE NATURE OF INCOMING MAIL:
Who Writes to Whom About What?

THE VOLUME OF MAIL

> There is a real danger that a senator's office may be swamped by a deluge of mail, for the overcrowded warrens where Senate staff members labor are already awash in seas of paper. (Moynihan 1981, p. 158)

While the dictum "write your congressman!" has no legal limits, there is a wide variation in who takes the time to communicate, what they concern themselves with, and whom they contact. Communicating with a member of Congress requires a certain amount of passion and knowledge concerning a cause, a feeling that the congressman has both the motivation and resources to change the course of events, and basic information on how and to whom to communicate. With each requirement, significant numbers of citizens are removed form the pool of potential communicators. For example, when only about 50 percent of U.S. citizens can spontaneously name their congressmen, at least half of the potential letter writers fail to fulfill the most basic requirement for initiating a communication.

Despite the inherent motivational and informational impediments, the U.S. citizenry cuts an impressive picture in its efforts to communicate with its congressmen. Depending on the wording of the pollster's question, anywhere from 10-25 percent of U.S. citizens have taken the opportunity to write their congressmen (Verba and Nie 1972, p. 353; Rosenau 1974, p. 66). In a 1978 survey, 7 percent of the respondents reported having contacted a member of Congress at least once for help in solving a problem, and 16 percent had written to express an opinion

9

or ask for information (Davidson 1981, p. 126). If one expands the criteria a bit to include not only those who have made direct contact with members of Congress but also those friends and relatives aware of their contact, the percentage increases to almost one-third of the population having some experience with contacting members of Congress (Powell 1982, p. 15). This translates to over 80 million pieces of incoming mail being handled by the congressional post offices each year (Kroger 1978, p. 37).

More important than the absolute figures is the growth in incoming mail. Both the percentage of citizens making demands on the Congress and the amount of mail generated have increased in recent decades. Figure 2.1 portrays vividly the increasing pressure of the mail on members of Congress.

Congressman Martin Dies highlights the change when he tells of his experiences:

> My father served in Congress from 1909 to 1919 from the state of Texas. During his last term I was one of his clerks. Congress sat for six months the first session and three months the second session. A Representative got about 15 letters a week...Most of a Member's time was spent on legislation. There was little else for him to do. (Congressman Martin Dies, quoted in Wright 1976, pp. 180–81)

Ten years after Congressman Dies made his comparison, the average House member was receiving over 600 letters per week (Johannes 1980, p. 655), with senators receiving at least double that amount.

A number of factors account for the increase in volume of incoming mail. The increase in congressional district population together with the spread of electoral competitiveness to the South has increased the number of potential communicators and heightened the motivation of future political candidates to serve these communicators' needs. The heightened political awareness spawned by affluence, increased education, and the spread of information through mass communication has increased the pool of constituents with the motivation and skills to communicate (Olson 1966, p. 345). Members are not innocent victims of increasing constituent demands. As one Member put it:

> You know how Members get that mail? They go back to their districts and talk up something, and then they get letters. Then they slay the dragon. But they've created that dragon they're going to slay....There are a lot of good actors around here. (quoted in Kingdon 1981, p. 57)

In the last few years, the volume of mail has swelled considerably due to the ability of interest groups to use targeted mailing lists for ''ad

FIGURE 2.1
THE VOLUME OF INCOMING CONGRESSIONAL MAIL

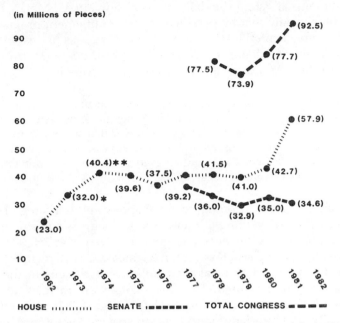

(in Millions of Pieces)

HOUSE ....   SENATE ....   TOTAL CONGRESS ━ ━ ━

NOTE: House figures are calculated by the U.S. Postal Service and do not include internal House communications or those from other government agencies. The figures underestimate constituent correspondence by counting bulk mail such as packets of postcards from organizations as one unit. Senate figures are not actual counts but Senate Post Office estimates and do include internal and interagency communications.

SOURCES:
*Olson 1966, p. 345.
*Ornstein et al. 1982, p. 141.

hoc constituency mobilization" (Keller 1982), a process where identifiable groups are noted, informed, and helped in writing their congressmen on an issue of concern to the interest group but not necessarily to members of the categoric group contacted (see Chapter 5). As one Capitol Hill observer noted:

> The nature of politics has changed drastically in the last few years, thanks to the growth of special interest groups with sophisticated, computer-directed mass-mailing drives which can generate thousands of letters and postcards to Congress on specific issues in a matter of days. (Himowitz 1982)

The most dramatic growth in incoming mail involves casework demands. This can be clearly accounted for by the virtual explosion of federal programs affecting the daily lives of individuals. Morris Fiorina argues convincingly that by passing complex entitlement programs which must be implemented by the bureaucracy, Congress has carved out a vital role as intermediator for dissatisfied constituents (Fiorina 1977 and 1981, passim). As Davidson and Oleszek describe it:

> Casework has burgeoned mainly to enhance incumbents' visibility and electoral support. . . . Congress enacts programs and creates bureaucracies with vague mandates, knowing full well that snags will arise when these services reach citizens. In turn, citizens ask elected officials to disentangle them, later showing their gratitude when reelection time rolls around. (Davidson and Oleszek 1981, p. 127)

While records of incoming mail are spotty and not categorized, some patterns are clear. Writing to members of Congress comes into focus as the result of historical events. Congress received over 350,000 telegrams after the firing of Special Prosecutor Archibald Cox (Green 1979, p. 308). The Watergate incident awakened millions of citizens to the utility of writing their congressmen. The sharp 26 percent increase in incoming mail volume between 1973 and 1974 (see Figure 2.1) makes this point graphically. The murder of John Lennon spawned emotional letters from thousands of younger citizens who had never before formally expressed an opinion on gun control (Moynihan 1981, p. 139). In 1983, with the help of postcards provided by banks opposed to government withholding of taxes on interest and dividends, the congressional mail volume was swelled from a normal 250,000 to over 800,000 pieces of incoming mail per day (Barker 1983), with the total volume of mail on the withholding issue adding up to over 20 million pieces. Experienced Capitol Hill staff members have learned that people take more time to write letters during the winter and after holidays (Hammond 1981, p. 205). One staff member argued:

> Bad weather has a lot to do with increasing the number of letters people write, and . . . there is always a predictable, generally supportive, surge in mail immediately following a television appearance by any president. (Moynihan 1981, p. 158)

WHAT DO THEY WRITE ABOUT?

So far we have treated all incoming mail alike, while in reality it varies dramatically in form and content. Table 2.1 summarizes two

TABLE 2.1
THE NATURE OF INCOMING CONGRESSIONAL MAIL

	1965 House Survey	1978 House Survey**
Issue mail	53%	47%
Casework requests	16%	29%
Federal grant requests	not defined	16%
Information requests	11%	28%
Other	20%	—

SOURCES:
Saloma 1969, p. 185.
**O'Donnell 1980, p. 10.

studies of mail arriving in congressional offices and reveals that while most communications still deal with the general legislation under consideration by the Congress, there has been a significant increase in casework mail. Congressmen are being asked more and more to focus their efforts on those particularized benefits which help individuals (casework and information requests) and on programs of particular benefit to a locality or group of individuals (help with federal grants).

WHO WRITES?

Communicating with a member of Congress largely exemplifies the general pattern that individuals with higher socioeconomic status (education, occupation, and income) tend to have the motivation and skills to participate in the political system.

Few Americans ever write their Congressmen. The highly educated, prosperous, and politically active are overrepresented. Constituents are more inclined to write to Congressmen with whom they agree than those with whom they take issue. (*Congressional Quarterly* 1976, p. 533)

Members of Congress have a legal constituency established by the state legislature, but more importantly they have an electoral constituency made up of actual voters, a supportive constituency comprised of those who voted for them, and an activist partisan constituency made up of those who contributed to their campaign with money, effort, or time. The closer a constituent is to being part of the activist partisan constituency, the more he is likely to communicate.

Contributors are much more likely than average citizens to make requests of their House member. Of those who had contributed to the incumbent 59% had contacted to express an opinion on a bill; 32% had contacted to express an opinion not on a bill; 46% had sought information; 34% had sought help on a problem...(Powell 1982, p. 13)

The general pattern relating socioeconomic status to an increased frequency of political communication applies most clearly to those constituents attempting to affect the stance of their congressmen on legislative issues.

The percentage of high income families in the district has a fairly large positive effect on members' tendency to take positions on national issues. The result is consistent with the hypothesized relationship; high income constituents, freed by affluence from dependence on government benefits, can afford to have their representatives pursue the ''larger issues'' of the day, issues which may produce long-term or distant benefits to them. (Yiannakis 1979, p. 16)

Above and beyond socioeconomic factors, issue contactors overrepresent whites, Protestants, and citizens living in rural areas and small towns. (Verba and Nie 1972, p. 119).

The conclusions concerning casework communications with members of Congress are considerably less clear. Based on national surveys during the early 1970s, Verba and Nie concluded that parochial contactors (those requesting casework) overrepresented a group of individuals lower on the socioeconomic status ladder and were also likely to be more urban, white, and Catholic (1972, p. 118). Later studies indicate that casework contactors are not much different from those contacting on issues:

The higher one's income, the more likely he or she is to make a casework request. It seems that the more one needs government aid, the less likely one is to ask...the poor are least likely of all those having problems with the government to be able to work their way through the bureaucratic labyrinth...they are, perhaps, also least likely to be aware that their representative is available to assist them....The affluent and well educated are more frequently exposed to situations in which casework is likely to be solicited...but even without such contacts, their greater political competence enables them to avail themselves of the casework services that their representatives provide. (Yiannakis 1981, pp. 574-75)

There is also some indication that those requesting casework come from the active partisan constituency of the congressman (Yiannakis 1981, p. 574; Powell 1982, p. 15), raising a question as to whether individuals seek out political involvement for the particularized benefits it can provide, or whether individuals once involved in politics become aware of the benefits they had been missing in the past.

Information plays an important part in determining whether an individual will target members of Congress as a possible solution to a problem. Individuals aware of what casework can do are clearly more likely to use it:

> Word of mouth, however, appears to be the strongest stimulus of demand for casework. People who have a friend who has received information or a favor from the member are most likely to make requests themselves. Thus, it appears that the more casework members do, the more they are asked to do, and (they hope) the more their electoral margins increase. (Yiannakis 1981, p. 574)

Determining who takes the initial step to use the resources of a congressional office to affect general policy or ameliorate personal problems is more than an academic exercise. If the current system only realistically receives communications from its better and/or more aware citizens, any hope for representing the needs of all citizens is greatly hampered. If particular groups within the population consistently miss the opportunity to express their needs in a system which tends to respond to those who make their wishes known, the stage is set for frustration and reduced faith in government.

WHO GETS THE MAIL?

Congressional offices are so bombarded with mail that their efforts go toward processing and answering it rather than counting and categorizing it. External studies of mail tend to be based on small samples and often focus on only certain types of communication. Studies of House offices indicate that the average office receives over 30,000 pieces of mail a year, with over 10,000 of them dealing with casework (Johannes 1980, p. 655). Some Senate offices receive over 1,000 letters per day with 70,000 cases per year (Cranston 1975, p. 17854; Davidson and Oleszek 1981, p. 125). Differences between one office and another can be dramatic. Congressman Stanley Lundine (D–NY) reported only 150 letters per week in 1975, while Morris Udall (D–AZ) had over 1,500 letters per week cross his mail handler's desk (Kroger 1978, p. 38). Particular events can increase the totals dramatically. In the ten days after President Reagan announced that he might cut Social Security benefits, Senator Moynihan (D–NY) received 37,071 letters on the issue (Moynihan 1981, p. 137). While the exact figures might be in doubt, no one questions the immensity of the burden constituent correspondence places on congressional offices nor the fact that the amount of correspondence has grown dramatically in recent years.

Given the larger size of their constituency and their higher visibility, it should come as no surprise that senators average more mail than members of the House. Within the Senate, though,

> mail does not vary systematically by state population. Some Senators from smaller states have a fairly heavy volume of mail. Other Senators from states with quite large populations have relatively small mail loads. And two Senators from the same state will have quite different mail loads. (Fox and Hammond 1977, p. 120)

Supporting the socioeconomic biases in individual propensity to write, it is clear that more mail comes from districts with higher socioeconomic status and from areas such as the Northeast, Florida, and California (Moynihan 1981, p. 136).

Congressmen with higher seniority and those who have received extensive publicity relating them to an issue or cause tend to get more mail than their more anonymous colleagues (Kroger 1978, p. 38). Seniority seems to increase constituent awareness of Members, and "familiarity breeds contacts" (Rundquist and Kellstedt 1982, p. 19). Members like Senator Kennedy (D–MA), who is a household name, receive over 70,000 casework requests per year (Breslin 1977, p. 21).

The volume of mail received by a congressional office does not stem simply from the static characteristics of the Member, office, or constituency. What comes into an office can be a result of careful efforts to pursue constituent complaints and opinions. Offices with an active outreach program (see Chapter 6) receive more mail than offices which sit back and react to what they naturally receive. This is especially true for casework. A recent study shows that

> The amount of time spent in the district [by the congressman] shows no relationship with expressing an opinion, a significant positive relationship with asking for information, and a significant stronger relationship with asking for help. (Powell 1982, p. 9)

Perhaps the best way to put the mail demands on U.S. congressmen in perspective is to compare them with other legislative bodies.

> The candid expression of opinion by Americans is unmatched in other Western democracies. In England, for example, a long-term member of Parliament, a member of the shadow cabinet, receives only about 150 letters per week. And in Sweden, one of the best-known and most

respected members of the Riksdag, the Swedish Parliament, gets only about 10 letters a week from individuals and seldom more than 25 from business firms. (Moynihan 1981, p. 165)

The average member of the British Parliament receives fewer than 50 letters per week, while over 50 percent of the German Bundestag members get fewer than 25 letters per week (Loewenberg and Patterson 1979, p. 175). Since observers of the U.S. Congress measure weekly mail counts in the hundreds and thousands, it is clear that the rush to express opinions and request help is unique to the U.S. political scene. With the deep constituent interest in beginning a mail dialog, it is no wonder that members of Congress view the mail as an important responsibility. Johannes (1984, p. 31) concludes that "seeking casework assistance from Congress, while limited to a small percentage of the citizenry, is more directly related to a constituent's political awareness...than to personal or demographic traits."

CHAPTER 3

THE CONGRESSIONAL RESPONSE

THE MOTIVATION TO COMMUNICATE

As the mail carts roll through halls of Congress five times a day—a good indication of the importance of mail in itself—Congressional offices stand primed to respond. The question is seldom "should we respond?" but rather "how can we respond most effectively?" Handling the mail is the prime responsibility in most offices. Other responsibilities often fall by the wayside, for getting behind on the correspondence one week causes an increasing problem as the mail from subsequent weeks adds to the existing delinquent pile. While the congressman and a few key aides may be able to insulate themselves from the crush of the mail and go on with their legislative tasks, the crush of incoming communications is an omnipresent reality for most of Capitol Hill.

The predisposition to respond to the mail stems from a mix of philosophical enlightenment and political reality. By and large, congressmen and the staffs they direct believe in their responsibility to represent, educate, and serve their constituents. Table 3.1 shows that while more congressmen see pure legislative activity as their primary goal, almost half of the respondents (48 percent) express a responsibility for service, representation, and education. These roles depend heavily on two-way communications. Members of Congress are acutely aware of the difficulty of establishing true communication in an era when Congress is in session nearly year-round.

Years ago, House members returned home for months at a time to live among their supportive constituencies, soak up the home atmosphere, and absorb local problems at first hand. Today, they race home for a

19

TABLE 3.1

LEGISLATIVE ROLES AS PERCEIVED BY MEMBERS OF
CONGRESS AND THE PUBLIC

Proper Emphasis for Legislators	Public Perception	Member Perception of Public Preference	Member Perception
Legislation	58%	87%	82%
Educational	41%	43%	3%
Constituency service	37%	79%	27%
Representation	35%	26%	18%
Bureaucratic oversight	1%	9%	41%

NOTE: Multiple responses accepted.

SOURCE: U.S., Congress, House. Commission on Administrative Review 1977, p. 865.

> day. . . . The citizen demand for access, for communication, and for the establishment of trust is as great as ever. So members go home. But the quality of their contact has suffered. "It's like a one-night stand in a singles bar." It's harder to sustain a genuine two-way communication than it once was. (Fenno 1978, p. 223)

With face-to-face communication less likely, the role of more indirect communications such as the mail looms larger.

Bolstering the internal commitment to communicate is the realization that the citizens on whom congressmen depend for political support have high expectations for the legislative roles which require frequent and meaningful communications. Whether one uses actual public expectations or congressional perceptions of those expectations (seeTable 3.1), it is clear that congressmen ignore communications at the peril of disappointing the public. While correctly perceiving general citizen interest in communicative public officials, congressmen, it is interesting to note, dramatically overestimate citizen interest in casework activity.

Congressmen get a great deal of advice and observe carefully the consequences of different behavior patterns. Numerous "Dutch uncle" talks by senior members to their more junior colleagues reveal the importance of handling the mail well:

> My experience is that people don't care how I vote on foreign aid, federal aid to education, and all those big issues, but they are very much interested in whether I answer their letters. (member of Congress, quoted in Green 1979, p. 239)

> Son, I have three pieces of advice for you if you want to stay in Congress. One, use the frank. Two, use the frank. Three, use the frank. (former congressman giving advice to his newly elected son, quoted in Green 1979, p. 276)

> Give close and prompt attention to your mail. Your votes and speeches may make you well known and give you a reputation, but it is the way you handle your mail that determines your reelection. (Speaker Bankhead to Estes Kefauver, quoted in Carlile 1981a, p. 9)

While incumbent congressmen seldom have difficulty in being reelected, it is the observation of insiders that those who do have lost touch with their districts. Effective communication is the accepted way of keeping in touch.

David Mayhew argues that most congressmen seek reelection above all other goals and that their success is premised on three activities: advertising (getting one's name out), credit claiming (being linked with positive policy or service outcomes), and position taking (being on the "right" side of issues of importance to your constituency.) Success in each of these areas depends more on the communication of a message than on the substance of the performance being communicated (Mayhew 1974, passim). Even an insider such as former Senator William Fulbright (D–AK) arugues that "the new breed of legislator, it seems, aims not to convey an idea but to project an image" (Fulbright 1979, p. 723). Whether the emphasis on communications is a new trend, or one we have only recently become aware of, the conclusion is the same: the two-way communication between congressmen and their constituents is important to all participants in the congressional process.

The motivation to communicate tends not to be selective, but leads to a general responsiveness:

> Members do not make tradeoffs between advertising and casework. Instead, incumbents who pay the most attention to their districts by spending a great deal of time at home, writing regular newspaper columns, and having regular radio or television programs also have more district offices, larger percentages of their staffs assigned to the district, and larger percentages of their staff members designated as caseworkers (Bond 1983, p. 15)

Highlighting the importance of the mail for congressional offices should not camouflage the variation between offices. Some of the variation stems from the idiosyncratic outlooks of the congressmen as to what roles they would like to play. More variation stems from the political realities. Members with secure electoral backgrounds have more freedom and thus need to please each individual constituent less. Research on the adoption of computers by members of the House to facilitate mail handling showed that electoral insecurity served as a primary stimulant to searching out new ways to satisfy felt needs (Frantzich 1982a, p. 201). Members from districts close to Washington can provide

more face-to-face communication and don't need to compensate with indirect methods such as the mail. Senators, with their larger constituencies, greater legislative responsibilities, and more ample staff, take much
less personal interest in the mail than do members of the House. While
there will always be variations, the increased perceived utility of an out-
standing communications approach is bound to raise the overall level of
commitment to the mail.

> We would expect a House member first elected by a narrow margin to
> place more importance on district attentiveness in his or her first term
> than would a member with a more secure beginning. Home styles, once
> established, tend to persist...in a situation of substantial uncertainty,
> why change a winning strategy? (Powell 1982, p. 5)

The congressional norm has become "the mail comes first." The variation among offices is more likely to be the degree to which they seek
to stimulate more mail, or go the step beyond simply responding to it
by using it to develop targeted mailing lists.

CONGRESSIONAL COMMUNICATIONS RESOURCES

Sensing the pressure to communicate, members of Congress have
structured their environment so as to respond to demands. Particularly
during the last few decades, congressmen have dramatically expanded
the resources necessary for handling the mail. To some degree, outside
demands led to an increased supply of resources. Simultaneously, the
supply of resources led to tactics for increasing the demand for communications and services. As one staff member described it:

> With the addition of staff and sophisticated equipment such as automatic
> typewriters, signature signing machines, and computers, we are not
> really ahead of the mail game; we have just worked that much harder
> to keep our heads above water so that we would not drown in the mail.
> Once we got the equipment, we couldn't justify having it stand idle,
> so we sought out new uses.

Staff

The story of mail handling is largely a story of staff. In the past, some
members of Congress took great pride in seeing every arriving letter, par-
ticipating in drafting a reply, and signing the final outcome. While some
congressmen still retreat from the constraints of the other duties of their
job by giving disproportionate personal attention to the mail (a realm

where they have more control over the outcome of their efforts), they are a dying breed (Dexter 1956, p. 18). Congressmen today do not have even perfunctory contact with the majority of their mail. They depend on staff to sort, count, prepare replies, and work the autopen machine. The congressman sees only a selection of the unique letters and perhaps a mail count on key issues. Stock responses are prepared based on the public record of the member. Only the most sensitive replies are drafted with the active participation of the member.

Senators are divorced even more from the mail handling process than are members of the House. Senate mail is often handled in "boiler room" operations physically removed from the main office in some cubbyhole annex. Numerous staff decisions have been made along the line before any letter makes it to the top staff members or the senators themselves. As one staff Member expressed it:

> I am rewarded not for what gets to the Senator, but for what he does not see. Our office uses the "ignorance is bliss" principle. The more we can effectively handle without help from the top, the better job we are doing.

Staff resources for the U.S. Congress have grown dramatically in recent decades (see Figure 3.1).

Among the committee and support agency staffs it is impossible to determine the amount of effort expended on constituent mail. Some units, such as the post office and folding rooms, exist for the mail. Other units, such as the computer systems' staffs, play a major role in facilitating mail. In other staffs the distribution of effort is even more difficult to determine. The Congressional Research Service, for example, which exists primarily to serve the research needs of Congress, handles over 50,000 constituent requests for information each year (Moynihan 1981, p. 159). Individual committee staffs help respond to constituency inquiries and communicate directly to the public.

It is a bit easier to determine the work patterns of each Member's personal staff. House members have a maximum of eighteen full-time staff members, which can be augmented by committee staff, interns, and part-time workers. The size of Senate staffs is based on the size of the state and varies from 20 to 40. Time studies of congressional offices (see Table 3.2) show that while congressmen spend only about 10 percent of their time dealing with constituent communications, the vast majority of staff time is spent on this task. House members with more limited staff make an "either/or" decision whether they will use staff for legislative or communications support, while Senators can "serve two masters" because of their larger staffs (Ornstein 1972, p. 172). Despite the level of

FIGURE 3.1
THE GROWTH OF CONGRESSIONAL STAFFS, 1891–1983

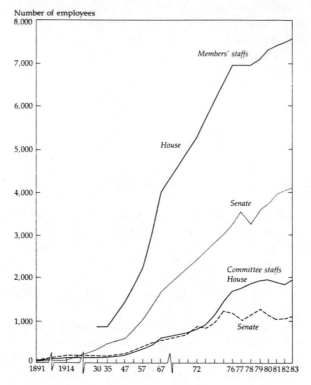

SOURCE: Ornstein, et al. 1984, p. 122. Reprinted by permission.

staff support, a recent survey of House members of the shortcomings of Congress as an organization revealed that the most common complaint (46 percent of those surveyed) was the understaffing of offices dealing with mail (Hammond 1981, p. 198). The importance of the staff comes into focus with a story told about a U.S. congressman touring the British House of Commons. Upon seeing the Library of Commons full of Members of Parliament writing to their constituents in longhand, the representative collapsed in shock (Crick 1965, p. 58).

Equipment

Although seldom at the forefront of technological innovation, Congress has been relatively quick to adopt new technology to handle its communications needs. Until the mid-1970s the major labor saving

TABLE 3.2
A PORTRAIT OF STAFF AND MEMBER EFFORT
(Percentage of Time Expended)

	Staff		Members	
Activity Areas	1969 House Study [a]	1977 House Study [b]	Senator Cranston's Office, 1975 [c]	1969 House Survey [d]
Legislation	14.3	13.9	12	49
Casework	24.7	26.9	not defined	9
Congressional mail	40.8	—	62	12
Other	20.2	—	26	30

SOURCES: [a]Saloma 1969.
[b]House Commission on Administrative Review Study, reported in Cavanaugh 1979, p. 238.
[c]Cranston 1975, p. S10137.
[d]Saloma 1969.

devices were the "robotype," which allowed duplicating letters as seemingly original copies, addressograph plates for mailing lists, and the "autopen," which created a seemingly original signature.

During the last decade, the name of the game has been computerization. Starting with tentative pilot projects which eventually led to system-wide applications, the Congress moved into the computer age. The House and the Senate took two different paths. The House used a decentralized approach, allowing members to use office funds to either purchase a commercial mail processing system or contract with outside vendors for the service. The Senate, on the other hand, initially established a central Correspondence Management System (CMS) and provided each senatorial office with a terminal. The Senate is currently changing course by providing offices with micro-computer networks and reserving the CMS system for mass mailings. Whatever the delivery system, computerization allows one to log incoming mail, create mail counts, place the names of communicators on coded mailing lists for future targeted mailing, create appropriate responses with interchangeable paragraphs, and establish a "tickler" system which reminds the staff member to check up on particular requests after a specified time. The vast majority of congressional offices currently use computers for a major portion of their communications (see Frantzich 1982a, passim).

Currently the average senatorial office has five terminals connected to the CMS system, each capable of sending out 40 "personalized" letters per hour, for a grand total of 2,500 letters per month. The Senate alone is sending out over a million letters per month with the CMS system, which means the average constituent could receive at least two such letters per year (Robinson 1981, p. 60). The advent of micro-computer networks for each office will expand the control, volume, and flexibility of senatorial mailings.

The Frank

Tremendous demands from constituents and extensive capacity to create sophisticated communications would mean little if members of Congress did not have the resources to get the mail out. The frank, the right to send mail out free over one's signature, provides the crucial resource for making extensive constituent communications feasible.

The right of legislators to free communication with their constituents was first claimed by the British House of Commons in 1660 and confirmed by statute in 1764 (Yadlosky 1981, p.3). In the United States, the Continental Congress first provided for the frank in 1775, and it has continued as a right of congressmen ever since, except for the period 1873–1895. Initially the frank allowed both free sending and receiving of mail by congressmen, but the burden of initiating a communication with a member soon became the responsibility of the constituent. (*Congressional Quarterly* 1979, p. 127).

The basic concept of the frank's role in improving congressional-constituency relations engenders little disagreement. The congressional response to a suit by Common Cause objecting to particular uses of the frank argued that:

> Historically, the premise that the use of the frank by Members of Congress serves a public interest has been almost universally accepted...The size of districts, distance from Washington and the length of session make it mandatory for members to use the mail to communicate to large, dispersed, distant and diverse constituencies...Congressmen have a need to communicate their views to the public and are entitled to fund the means to accomplish this communication. (Yadlosky and Bird 1981, pp. 7–8)

In the early days of the Republic, two of the founding fathers, Jefferson and Madison, took a strong stand against any restriction, upholding the right of a congressman to write letters critical of the President:

> In order to give to the will of the people the influence it ought to have, and the information which may enable them to exercise it usefully...their [The representatives'] communications with their constituents should of right, as of duty also, be free, full and unawed by any...the correspondence between representative and constituent is privileged there to pass free of expense through the channel of the public post." (Kennedy 1980, p. 733)

The operative term for determining what could be sent under the frank has always been "official business." Prior to 1973, no statutory regulations as to the proper use of the frank existed and members were expected to use common sense in sorting out personal mail, campaign communications, and official business. As might be expected in an institution with diverse perspectives and ethical standards, individual criteria varied. Until 1973, congressmen turned to the Post Office Department for interpretive rulings and advisory opinions as to the frankability of materials under the "official business" test. Realizing the untenability of overseeing the branch of government responsible for its funding, and after failing in its attempt to get Senator Griffith (R-MI) to repay $25,000 for newsletters it judged to be too political, the Post Office Department gave in, refusing to give advisory opinions or make judgements. It conceded that the use of the frank was "a matter strictly between the member of Congress and their conscience" (Green 1979, p. 160).

Growing criticisms of the frank centered around both the growing cost of congressional mailings (see Table 3.3) and the perception that the frank was being used increasingly for political self-promotion rather than educating constituents.

Some misuse was rather flagrant, with newsletters virtually soliciting campaign funds and mailings doing little but touting the incumbent. Other approaches showed more creativity in using seemingly legitimate methods of gaining political advantage. The *Congressional Record* was always viewed as a legitimate expression of the official business of Congress and therefore frankable:

> Representative Alvin O'Konski prepared for his 1972 reelection campaign by sending a flood of material into the *Record* in December, 1971 (long enough before the election that it would not become a campaign issue)—including the "Biography of Alvin E. O'Konski" and an impressive list of his successes in supping from the pork barrel. (Green 1979, p. 277)

In 1973, Congress bit the bullet and began restricting by statute the use of the frank. In order to stem the most flagrant abuses, members were not allowed to send mass mailings two months prior to an election; were not allowed to solicit funds using the frank; could not send unofficial communications (Christmas cards, sympathy cards, or letters of congratulation) under the frank; and had to limit the number of pictures and uses of the pronoun "I" in their newsletters.

While the new legislation solved some problems, lack of strick enforcement and the human capacity to circumvent the spirit of the laws while upholding the letter provided a great deal of room for potential

TABLE 3.3
OFFICIAL CONGRESSIONAL MAILING COSTS, 1971–1984

Year	Appropriations (dollars)	Average Unit Cost of Franked Mail (cents)
1971	11,244,000	8
1972	14,594,000	8
1972 supplement	18,400,000	—
1973	21,226,480	8.79
1974	30,500,000	9.9
1975	38,756,015	11.4
1976	46,101,000	13.2
Transition period[a]	11,525,000	—
1976 supplement	16,080,000	—
1977	46,904,000	13.4
1978	48,926,000	12.7
1979	64,944,000	13.98
1980[b]	50,707,000	13.39
1981	52,033,000	—
1982	75,095,000	13.94[c]
1983	93,161,000	12.3[c]
1984	107,077,000	12.3[c]

[a]Reflects change in the fiscal year from July 1 to October 1.
[b]Lower figure reflects decrease in bulk mail rates.
[c]Estimate.

NOTE: 1984 figure does not include supplementals.

SOURCE: Ornstein et al. 1984, p. 131. Reprinted by permission.

misuse. The 60-day limit on mass mailings quickly became a target date for all congressional offices. Newsletters, constituent polls, and the like became timed to arrive in the folding room just under the 60-day limit. The halls surrounding congressional mail rooms became huge warehouses for mountains of mail, all of which met the legal limit of being "mailed" sixty days before the election, but most of which would not be processed for many days or weeks. It was not unknown for offices to send down staff members to the storage area to put their mail carts at the back of the line in hopes of delaying its arrival by a few days and thereby reaping more name identification closer to the election. Other Members have used mass-mailing techniques exempted by the rules. Members are allowed to send town-meeting notices at any time under the rationale that the constituency is served by having contact with the legislator at any time. It is often difficult to distinguish between a town meeting with an incumbent congressman and a campaign rally. Using the town-meeting notice loophole, one member turned circumventing the intention of the law into an art form and campaigned up to election day. Realizing that form may be more important than substance in constituent communications, this Member organized his mailing list by the amount of time it took to get a letter from Washington. He then sent out meeting notices for every Saturday morning up to election day late enough in the week so that they would arrive in the Saturday morning mail. He would show up for the early morning session before most of the target audience got their notice. The constituent going to the mail box at 11 a.m. would be greeted with the notice that the congressman had been at the town hall from 8–10 that morning. Rather than getting angry at the congressman, the constituent would damn the inefficient postal service while simultaneously crediting the congressman with trying to keep in touch. Without having to face a horde of constituents with its demands, requests, and desire for explanations, he got all the credit and little of the hassle.

Opposition to the more political use of the frank solidified around a suit brought by Common Cause, self-styled citizens' lobby. First filed in 1974, the suit argued that particular mailings such as mass newsletters, press releases, material laudatory to the Member, and mailings to citizens outside the Member's district did not constitute "official business" and provided a substantial benefit to incumbents running for re-election:

> Briefly summarized, the constitutional issues raised in the COMMON CAUSE suit are that the authorization for the use of the frank by 39 U.S.C. #3210 for mass mailed newsletters and news releases under the frank after Members of Congress have announced their candidacy for nomination or election abridged the First and Fifth Amendment rights of Plantiffs freely to associate for the purpose of advancing political beliefs and supporting political parties and candidates for Federal elective office by conferring a substantial political benefit upon Members of Congress who are candidates for Federal elective office while not conferring the same benefits upon candidates for those offices who are not Members of Congress. (Yadlosky and Maskell 1980, p. 7)

As the technology of computerized targeted mailings became available, Common Cause expanded its criticisms to the right of congressmen to purchase and process mailing lists with federal funds and use the frank to mail to people on these lists.

In its denial of the Common Cause position, the district court concluded:

We do not suggest that the franking privilege may never be shown to create such an imbalance in the campaign process as to constitute a cognizable interference with important rights. We hold only that the level of impact has not been shown to be sufficient in this case for us to assume the responsibility of redrafting a statute or promulgating regulations to govern the congressional use of the frank.(quoted in Yadlosky 1982, p. 6)

Partially as a result of the Common Cause suit, Congress tightened up its franking regulations ir 1981 by lengthening the preelection cutoff for mass mailings to 60 days, outlawing the use of campaign money to supplement mass-mailing allowances, and restricting mass mailings to Members' districts if they were running for statewide office (Maskell 1981, p. 5). In 1982, the Common Cause suit was dismissed after eight years of review.

Traditionally, the House and Senate have differed on one major aspect of using the frank. House members can use postal patron mailings to contact every member of their constituency six times a year (or they can cover particular portions of their constituency more than six times if they drop other sections). The average member of the House sends four newsletters a year to his average 170,000 postal patrons (Perdue 1977, p. 52). Senators, on the other hand, must send all mass mailings to specific addressees, which means tremendous efforts at mailing list creation and real limits on the number of constituents who can be contacted.

While the direct costs of congressional mailings are easy to estimate (see Table 3.3), it is more difficult to estimate the indirect costs and, most importantly, match the value of communications to the cost. The indirect costs come in many forms. Aside from the frank, the average House member spends over $10,000 per year on envelopes and stationery, while receiving an equal amount in free government publications which can be showered on constituents (Perdue 1977, p. 52). Senators are supposed to be limited in their mailings by being allotted only one piece of paper per constituent per year; but ready transfer of paper allotments from one year to the next and from one senator to another means that few communications have been thwarted by a lack of paper to print them on. The total cost of the folding rooms and the partial cost of the printshops and computer operations must be chalked up against the mailing ledger. Legislative liaison offices and office caseworkers who deal with constituent problems have been estimated to cost a minimum of $40 million per year (Breslin 1977, p. 30). The Department of Agriculture alone spends over $1 million per year to provide congressmen with free gift books for constituents (Pincus 1977c, p. a4). Even more indirectly, virtually every congressional staff member exerts some effort in keeping the mail moving, and numerious congressmen use some of their limited time to deal with the mail.

Considerations of the direct and indirect costs of congressional mailings force one to compare the large and growing costs with an evaluation of the value of congressional mail. While no one argues for an isolated and noncommunicative Congress, the heavy emphasis on mail raises many questions as to whether mail volume, especially unsolicited outgoing mail, places too heavy a burden on both congressional offices and the taxpayer. Senator Mathias (R–MD), chairman of the Senate Rules and Administration Committee, which oversees the frank and mailing procedures, is particularly concerned about the fact that only 4 percent of outgoing senatorial mail relates to a direct request from a constituent:

> The mass mailings, those things we generate ourselves, with our pictures in them, our names prominently displayed, will total 245 million pieces of mail this year—11 million which we are responding to constituents; 245 million that we are casting out to the winds. (Mathias 1982a, p. S11333)

One's judgement as to the value of congressional mail depends to a large degree on the importance one attaches to developing a two-way communications flow and one's prediction whether reducing the emphasis on the mail would allow congressmen and their staffs more time and resources for legislative work.

The uniqueness of the administrative and communications burden of members of the U.S. Congress—as opposed to their deliberative duties—comes into focus by comparing their office resources to those of their counterparts in the British House of Commons. While British MPs have constituencies one-sixth the size of those served by members of Congress, they have one-thirtieth the personal staff help, share small offices, and do not have the frank. (Ranney 1981, p. 69).

So while the U.S. Congress may be inundated with both incoming and outgoing mail, it has favored itself with a relatively efficient structure and adequate resources to handle the volume. The congressional mail handling resources in many ways resemble those of a large mail-order firm.

MAIL HANDLING STRATEGIES

The basic approach in every office is to view all incoming letters as deserving a response. Increasingly, and especially in the Senate, the first step a letter goes through is a sorting and information-gathering process. Sitting in front of a computer terminal, a staff member scans every letter for subject matter and information on the writer, which is then transferred to a mailing list. This list can then be called on later to develop specialized targeted mailing lists for people who have written on a particular subject, constituents from a specific area, individuals with a certain ethnic name, and the like. The letter then is routed to a caseworker or a legislative assistant dealing with a particular policy area.

Most offices have a file for "kook" letters which make ridiculous claims or demands: "Dear Mr. Congressman, My breakfast cereal is being bugged by the CIA. What are you going to do about it?" The first letter is usually answered seriously, but as a pattern of constant harassment develops, the letters are not replied to (see Chapter 8 for further examples).

Casework is a special topic and will be dealt with in the next chapter. Legislative mail expressing an opinion on current policy issues provides a special challenge (see Chapter 5 for more details). On issues where only a few people write, original letters are drafted on each issue. Once an issue elicits numerous requests, most offices create a standard letter or a series of stock paragraphs which can be assembled automatically, using a computer or automatic typewriter. While some would argue that automating the mail reduces personalization, a strong case can be made for the argument that a higher quality response truly reflecting the views of the congressman is more likely when the congressman and his staff take the time to develop a well-crafted letter and that it makes little sense to tie up valuable staff time repeatedly drafting minor revisions of a standard theme.

A great deal of mail arriving in a congressional office is misdirected. Congressmen are often asked to deal with problems well outside their legal purview (i.e. fix the potholes in my street, help me speed up my driver's license application, help repeal the city curfew, etc.). Most offices will respond to such requests, expressing their sympathy and redirecting the constituent to the proper authorities. Similar misdirection occurs when a Member receives letters from another congressman's constituents. As Congressman Morris Udall advises, these letters are usually sent to the proper office with a "buck slip":

Members frequently receive mail from persons residing in other congressional districts. Such mail is customarily forwarded to the member who represents the district in which the writer lives. There are three general exceptions to the rule: If the subject matter specifically relates to the member to whom the letter is addressed; If the reason for writing him is that he has special competence in the subject matter; or if the writer gives a sound reason for not contacting their own Representative. (Tacheron and Udall 1970, p. 82)

The willingness of Members to take on nondistrict communications often provides a subtle hint as to their political ambitions. Before attempting a run for the Senate, many House members will instruct their staff to begin servicing communications from anyone in the state. More aggressive candidates will let the word out that they are ready and willing to start a dialogue with a wider constituency. Candidates for the presidency fortunate enough to be holding congressional office regularly use the frank to explain their stands on issues to anyone who requests information.

Traditionally, a congressman's Washington office served as the hub of the constituent communications operation, if for no other reason than to maintain the facade that incoming letters would be in close proximity to the member and would therefore be more likely to garner some of his attention. Increasingly, congressmen are shifting much of their communications efforts back to their district offices. For many Members, the vast majority of casework occurs back in the district, as well as most of the routine issues communications. With the increased use of computer-generated responses, it makes little difference whether the printer is in Washington or Idaho. Senator Mark Hatfield (R–OR) uses the Correspondence Management System to have virtually all of his constituent letters printed and distributed from his district offices, thereby speeding up delivery by two or three days.

While a few Members still sign all their mail, the norm is to use technology to reduce the drudgery, especially when one is dealing with a mountain of redundant communications. Such technological aids have been around for a number of years, as evidenced by the comments of former Senator Joseph Clark in the 1960s:

My signature is reproduced, or forged if you will, to practically all my letters by a device known as an "autopen"—a wonderful product of automation which saves precious hours each week. There are three forged signatures. Most answers get the formal "Joseph S. Clark." Politicians who are not intimate get "Joe Clark."Friends get "Joe," as do a fair number who are not friends but call me "Joe" when they write. (Clark 1964, p. 60)

Only recently, however, has the majority of Members felt free to admit that every single letter did not get personal and undivided attention.

THE VOLUME OF MAIL

Overall Volume

One look at Figure 3.2 seems to indicate that constituents have an insatiable appetite for congressional communications and congressmen an unbridled desire to satisfy the hunger. Between 1960 and 1980, the volume of outgoing pieces increased almost 500 percent. The largest increases occured in the late 1970s as computerization facilitated both the creation of personalized letters and the rapid addressing of printed mass communications.

Variations and Cycles

Overall measures of volume tend to paper over some predictable patterns and cycles. The clearest pattern involves election year surges and off-year slumps in mail volume.

FIGURE 3.2
THE VOLUME OF CONGRESSIONAL FRANKED MAILINGS,
1919–1983
(In Millions of Pieces)

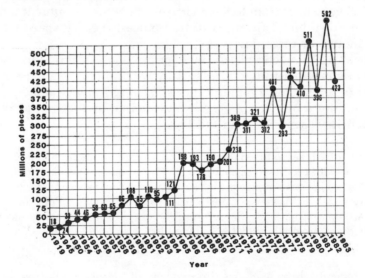

SOURCES: 1919, Cover 1980, p. 125; 1945-51, *Congressional Quarterly* 1976, p. 13; 1954–1983, Ornstein et al. 1984, p. 152.

The annual folding room workload follows a regular cycle of even year peaks and odd year troughs...the end of a Congress (the even year) generally marks the beginning of intensive pre-election campaigning....Clearly members were not waiting until the last minute to conclude congressional business before reporting back to constituents....Many members presumably chose a politically opportune time to communicate. (Cover 1976, pp. 20–21)

As is graphically clear in Figure 3.2, outgoing mail volume grew at a steady, almost linear, rate until the early 1960s. From that point on, and especially after the early 1970s when computerized mail operations became the norm, dramatic fluctuations in overall outgoing mail volume coincided with the election year cycle. Output in an election year raised the off-year volume to a higher plateau than the previous nonelection year. This election-year surge is particularly true for unsolicited mass mailings as opposed to responses to individual requests for help or information, as is clear from Figures 3.3 and 3.4.

Variations in volume of outgoing mail from individual congressional offices depend on such factors as constituency characteristics (size, po-

FIGURE 3.3
ELECTION AND NONELECTION YEAR VARIATION IN HOUSE MASS MAILINGS

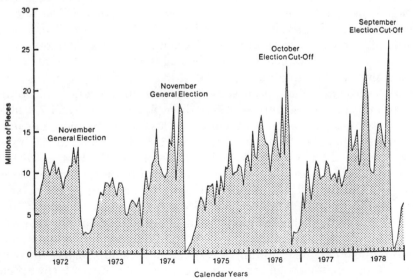

SOURCE: Common Cause 1981 (Unpublished court motion).

FIGURE 3.4
VARIATION IN MASS MAILINGS AMONG SENATORS IN THE CLASSES OF 1974, 1976, AND 1978

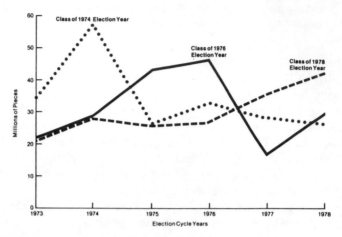

SOURCE: Common Cause 1981 (unpublished court motion).

litical awareness, perceived needs, the existence of local instigators, etc.), the role perceptions of the member, and particularly political needs. While comprehensive data on mailing volume by individual office are a closely kept secret, it is clear that Members in electoral difficulty communicate more frequently than Members who feel secure. This is dramatically pointed out in Figure 3.4, where it is seen that senators facing an election threat produce much more mail than their colleagues not in a campaign. Although atypical, some of the extremes in mailing effort point out how much emphasis some Members put on communications. In a recent year one senator sent 6 million pieces of mail to 1.7 million mailboxes, while the average senator sent less than one piece per mailbox to his or her state (Mathias 1982a, p. S11333). In 1981, thirteen senators accounted for over one-half the mail sent out (Mathias 1982b). In the House, the vast majority of Members send out over three newsletters per year (Haskell 1982, p. 49), while some Members send twelve or more a year to the 150,000 or so mailboxes in the typical district.

For the individual constituent, total volume figures mean relatively little, since certain constituents on the correct mailing lists may be inundated while others hear nothing. Despite the variation, voters' recollections about receiving mail in recent elections point out both the spread of constituent mail and the advantage it gives the incumbents. In 1978, 71 percent of the voters remembered getting mail from the House incumbent and only 16 percent from the challenger. In the Senate, 53 percent reported mail from the incumbent and 32 percent from the challenger (Cover & Brumberg 1982, p. 248).

What Goes Out

Using the general term "mail" to describe what emanates from congressional offices clouds some important distinctions between kinds of communications. Clearly, the largest volume of outgoing mail, and that which has grown most dramatically (see Figure 3.5), falls in the category of unsolicited mass mailings composed of newsletters, town meeting notices, and press releases sent to postal patrons by House members and to established mailing lists by Members of both chambers. A recent study in the Senate indicated that 69 percent of the outgoing mail was composed of newsletters, 23 percent of town meeting notices and other mass mailings, and 8 percent at most of individualized issue or casework mail (Mathias 1982a, p. S11334).

The ready adaptability of modern technology for more efficient and effective mass communications and mailing list utilization means that there are few physical limitations to continued expansion of this type of communications (see Chapters 6 and 9).

So far we have dealt with incoming and outgoing communications as separate phenomena, and we have implied by the ordering of the

FIGURE 3.5
INCREASE IN SENATE MASS MAILINGS, 1979-1982
(in millions of pieces)

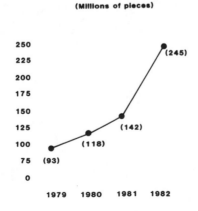

(Millions of pieces)

250
225
200
175
150
125 (142)
100 (118)
75 (93)
0

1979   1980   1981   1982

(245)

SOURCE: Mathias 1982a, p. S11332.

chapters that, if anything, incoming communications have much more impact on outgoing communications than vice versa. While congressional offices do respond to outside demands, what goes out of a congressional office has a major influence on what comes in as well. Congressmen who develop a reputation for dealing effectively with constituent complaints, who deal seriously with their issue mail, and/or who solicit communications through their newsletters and other forms of advertisement are likely to find their demands from constituents increasing. It can become a vicious circle of gearing up for incoming communications and meeting the challenge, only to have the newly generated demands requiring a redoubled effort. The continued escalation is fueled by the perception (and probable reality) that effective two-way communications between congressmen and their constituents is the best way to secure one's political future.

CHAPTER 4

DEALING WITH CASEWORK DEMANDS

All God's chillun got problems (former Congressman Billy Matthews, quoted in Davidson and Oleszek 1981, p. 125)

A Congressman has become an expanded messenger boy, an employment agency, getter-out of the Navy, Army and Marines, a ward heeler, a wound healer, trouble shooter, law explainer, bill finder, issue translator, resolution interpreter, controversy-oil-pourer, glad-hand extender, business promoter, veteran's affairs adjuster, ex-serviceman's champion, watchdog for the underdog, sympathizer for the upperdog, kisser of babies, recoverer of lost baggage, soberer of delegates, adjuster for traffic violations...contributor to good causes, cornerstone layer, public building and bridge dedicator and ship christener. (Congressman Luther Patrick, quoted in Evins 1963, p. 18)

People turn to their congressman or senator for help when the rest of the system fails. They don't vote for the Small Business Administration, or the Farmer's Home Director, or the EDA Assistant Secretary. They probably never see them. They don't vote for the Social Security Administrator. They do vote for their congressman and senator. They see them, know them, touch them, talk to them, write to them. (Cavanaugh 1981, p. 66)

Constituent work: that's something I feel very strongly about. The American people, with the growth of the bureaucracy, feel nobody cares. The only conduit a taxpayer has with the government is a congressional office. (congressman, quoted in Cavanaugh 1981, p. 65)

''Dear Mr. Congressman: Help! I have tried everyone else and you are my last hope.'' Variants of this message flow into congressional offices by the thousands each day. While a congressman's job is often idealized to include only deliberating over issues of national importance, constituents frequently look to their representatives for other reasons.

> In recent years, legislators have begun to get out of the business of legis-
> lating. In economic parlance, they have begun to diversify. The reason
> is simple: there are incentives for the supply of services other than legis-
> lative. Congressional entrepreneurs have become convinced of some-
> thing that courthouse politicians and ward heelers have known for
> years—that for most people, most of the time, politics means something
> other than passing laws. The electorate is most concerned with the
> things that hit closest to home. By heeding the widespread demand for
> constituency service, members can improve their position in the elec-
> toral arena. By stimulating the demand for these services, members can
> strengthen their positions even more. (Cavanagh 1979, p. 241)

Constituency service or "casework" eschews primary concern for broad, universalistic issues of public policy and instead focuses on particularized benefits. Such benefits exhibit two characteristics: (1) each benefit is given out to a specific individual or an identifiable small group, and (2) the perceived rules for distribution do not entitle every petitioner automatic benefits but require special intervention (see Mayhew 1977, pp. 53–54). The "casework" terminology comes from the fact that each request is handled on a case-by-case basis, with little concern for the broader implications of such piecemeal policy making. In such situations, the congressman can earn the gratitude of constituents by agreeing to intervene and providing selective benefits to those who bother to ask. Such gratitude is more potent than a constituent's appreciation for a stand on national legislation, since the constituent feels that he has direct access and is getting his individual share of government service.

While we will see that casework has grown dramatically in both volume and variety, its origin stems back to the early days of representative government. The use of elected representatives to intervene on behalf of their constituents to secure the redress of their constituents' grievances against government appears as early as 1215 in the Magna Charta, when King John of England at Runnymede granted his barons the right to "keep and cause to be observed, the liberties which we have granted."

THE NATURE OF CASEWORK DEMANDS

If a constituent can link a personal problem to government in even the most tangential or logically convoluted way, there is a good chance his demand will eventually end up in his congressman's office. Many constituents write their congressmen less out of a conviction that their problems lie directly within the realm of the congressmen's responsibilities than out of frustration in not knowing where to direct their requests or after getting caught in the bureaucratic labyrinth and coming out unsatisfied. While everyone would agree that the congressional office should deal with virtually any government-related problem if all other more direct approaches have been exhausted, it is clear that many constituents attempt to short-circuit the system by approaching their congressmen as a first rather than last resort.

Casework for Individual Constituents

Individual constituents appeal to congressional offices for two basic types of help: (1) information and (2) bureaucratic intervention. Information requests are generally quite straightforward and pose little difficulty. A constituent planning a trip to Washington might write for maps, guidebooks, and calendars of special events. Most offices have developed a tourist packet, and some groups (such as the Republican Congressional Committee) have even seen the political benefits of satisfying constituent visitors and developed a comprehensive handbook to be given out by party members. A constituent writing of his interest in a specific area of public policy might find in the return mail a packet of committee reports or excerpts from floor speeches by the Member. Students researching government-related subjects often request help from congressional offices, who in turn call on the Congressional Research Service in the Library of Congress. Although designed to serve the research needs of the Congress, the CRS maintains hundreds of general briefing packets which can be requested and distributed by members of Congress. Over 50,000 information requests for constituents were handled by the CRS in 1981.

While the demands of the congressional workload mitigate against comprehensive monitoring and categorizing of incoming case mail, current Member and staff perceptions match the results found by Gellhorn in the mid-1960s (Gellhorn 1966; Johannes 1984, p. 245). About one-quarter of the casework mail in a typical office involves information requests (see Figure 4.1).

By far the greater challenge for the congressional office involves individual requests for intervention in the bureaucratic process. The variety of concerns brought to the congressman's attention runs the gamut of areas where the government intersects with individual lives. Any listing of examples touches only the surface of the variety and complexity of the requests:

FIGURE 4.1
VARIETIES OF INCOMING CONGRESSIONAL CASEWORK

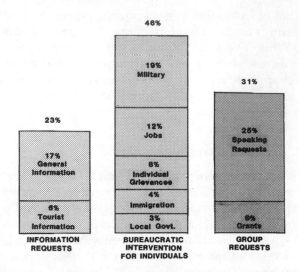

SOURCE: Gellhorn 1966, pp. 63–64.

A civilian employee at a military installation was injured by a meat grinder and received an official reprimand without a hearing. In hopes of getting a promotion, he wanted to get this off his record. Two years of efforts on his own did no good. One letter from the congressman changed the decision.

A man requested a full military funeral for his brother, a decorated veteran, but was denied the request because the color guards were gone for Christmas vacation. Nine calls from the congressional office later and a guard was finally found (reported by Congressman Clarence Long [D-MD] 1964, p. 21480).

A woman with a 90-year-old mother in Hungary got her congressman to sponsor a private bill allowing the mother into the country despite the fact that she did not fit under the immigration quota.

A veteran whose disability checks stopped when he moved gave up trying to straighten out the problem with the Veteran's Administration and turned to his congressman for help.

Requests for bureaucratic intervention cover the entire continuum from cases where the government was clearly wrong and the congressman is asked to rectify the situation, to cases where the desire is to speed up a decision, to cases where the constituent wants unwarranted preferment. As Figure 4.1 reveals, a large percentage of cases involves entering, escaping, or changing the conditions of military service. While such requests still tax congressional offices, the dropping of the draft has probably reduced the percentage of these cases in recent years. While job seekers comprise a large percentage of constituent requests, such cases receive relatively little attention in most offices and generate little more than a polite letter of commiseration and perhaps a general pamphlet or two on job hunting. Individual grievances and help with immigration problems, while a smaller percentage of the total requests, often involve crucial issues concerning a constituent's future or happiness and take up a considerable amount of staff time. Some incoming requests are clearly out of the realm of responsibility of members of Congress and typically lead to a letter redirecting the constituent to the proper state or local government office; or, in the case of members with a deep casework commitment, such requests may spur an attempt to intervene at another level of government.

Group Casework: The Allocation of Time, Government Grants and Contracts

Increasingly, as the federal government has shown special interest in various programs through funding selected applications and has become a major consumer of goods and services, congressmen have been called on to look out for the interests of local governments, civic groups, and business concerns within their districts. Such "high-level casework" (see Westin 1973, p. 69) involves congressmen and their staffs with some of the most highly motivated and politically active individuals in their constituencies.

The initial group demand on the congressman often comes in the form of a speaking request. The local chamber of commerce, teachers' union, or association of mayors may simply want some information on what is happening in Washington or may wish to affect the course of legislation; but in many cases the speaking engagement is to lay the groundwork for later requests for help in receiving a government grant or securing a government contract for goods or services for a local business. Most Members shepherd their time quite carefully, attempting to accept only those speaking engagements which afford them the most exposure to the most useful groups (see Fenno 1978, p. 106).

When it comes to securing specific government grants and contracts, the congressman can facilitate the process. At the legislative stage, congressmen often battle over eligibility criteria to allow their constituents a better chance for selection. In general, members of Congress prefer programs based on pilot projects or a limited number of project grants to

programs based on open-ended entitlement programs where anyone ful-
filling the criteria receives the benefit, since under the former they are
part of the selection process and can claim some credit.

In the selection process, Members offer to help in any way possible.
When the local school superintendent calls to get government help to re-
place a burned-out science wing of the high school, the congressional office helps find the appropriate programs, sends out the application
forms, accompanies the local officials when they make their case in
Washington, publicly announces the grant, and expresses its willingness
to have the congressman at the ribbon-cutting ceremony naming the new
facility after him.

THE VOLUME OF CASEWORK DEMANDS

As the mail trucks disgorge their contents on congressional offices
each day, over one-half of the mail will involve some type of casework
(see Table 2.1). While the volume varies dramatically from one office to
the next, several studies, focusing on somewhat different time periods
and using different definitions, conclude that the average congressional
office receives between 100 and 200 casework requests per week (Gellhorn 1966, p. 63; U.S. Congress, House, Commission on Administrative Review 1977, p. 655; Johannes 1981, p. 79; Moynihan 1981, p. 137;
Johannes 1984, p. 35). With such a weekly volume, the average congressional office must currently process 10,000 or more cases per year. While
offices vary dramatically in volume, there are few clear patterns. By and
large the volume of casework is not related to district characteristics such
as education, income, party, and other indirect measures of awareness
and possible need for services (Johannes 1981, p. 540; Verba and Nie
1972, p. 132). This makes some intuitive sense since the characteristics
associated with general political participation and awareness of Congress
as a target for government help are not related to those social characteristics leading to more intense need for government aid. The only district
characteristic consistently associated with variation in casework demands
is size, with senators from large states receiving many more requests (Johannes 1981, p. 540). There is also some evidence that individuals are
more likely to approach a member of the House, while groups seeking
grants or contacts will focus their efforts on the Senate (Gellhorn 1966,
p. 66). Much variation in the number of casework demands stems from
the tradition of commitment to service and actual success created by the
incumbent and passed through the constituency via word of mouth or
active congressional solicitation. The other major variation involves
seniority. More experienced legislators tend to get more casework re-

quests than their junior colleagues (U.S. Congress, House, Commission on Administrative Review 1977, p. 655). This could mean either that constituents perceive the value of experience and leadership positions for dealing with the bureaucracy and have higher expectations of such members, or that senior members have gained consistent reelection through a greater than average commitment to casework service.

The absolute figures on casework clearly underrepresent the number of citizens having difficulty with government, since a large percentage of the population lacks either the motivation or knowledge to use its congressional office. On the other hand, the figures also overrepresent the number of discrete problems being dealt with. Most constituents hedge their bets and duplicate their requests to their representatives and one or two senators (Gellhorn 1966, pp. 65–66).

Casework Growth

While observers differ on the nuances of the levels and causes of variation in casework load, they do agree on the dramatic pattern of across-the-board growth in requests over the last few decades. One long-time observer asserted that casework had doubled in the decade between 1967 and 1977 (Johannes, quoted in U.S. Congress, House, Commission on Administrative Review 1977, p. 655).

A number of factors stand out as explanations for the growth. Citizens have increased their opinion that they as individuals have the right to make demands on government directly. As Senator William Cohen (R–ME) explained the change:

Over the past several decades casework has undergone two fundamental changes. Until the 1960's, the manner in which congressmen first learned of constituents' problems was usually indirect. A family needing help would first appeal to a local politician or religious leader, who would in turn get in touch with the congressman. The screening at the local level provided a useful verification that grievances were legitimate. But times have changed; now people feel closer to their elected representatives... The screening of most cases today must therefore be at the staff level. (Cohen 1982, p. 14)

Associated with this heightened sense of opportunity is a broadened definition of responsiveness to clearly include constituent service. As one congressional administrative assistant said, "The whole concept of representation has changed in the last ten years. People don't just want their congressman voting, they demand service. If they have a problem...they write" (Kroger 1978, p. 38). Perhaps the greatest factor increasing casework demands has less to do with changed attitudes than with the reality that the complexity and pervasiveness of government intersects more and more with our daily lives. In the not so distant past, the postal service was the average American's only daily contact with government. Today, through regulation, provision of services, entitlement allocations, and the like, our lives are regularly intertwined with the decisions and performance of the national government. With more contact, citizens simply have more chances for things to go wrong in their relationship with government, and thus they need more help.

Morris Fiorina argues cogently that congressmen are neither victims nor simply bystanders in this development, but rather are co-conspirators in the plot and benefit by it:

> Congressmen (typically the majority Democrats) earn electoral credits by establishing various federal programs (the minority Republicans typically earn credits by fighting the good fight). The legislation is drafted in very general terms, so some agency, existing or newly established, must translate a vague policy mandate into a functioning program, a process that necessitates the promulgation of numerous rules and regulations, and incidentally, the trampling of numerous toes. At the next stage, aggrieved and/or hopeful constituents petition their congressman to intervene in the complex (or at least obscure) decision process of the bureaucracy. The cycle closes when the congressman lends a sympathetic ear, piously denounces the evil of bureaucracy, intervenes in the latter's decisions, and rides a grateful electorate to ever more impressive electoral showings. Congressmen take credit both coming and going. (Fiorina 1977, p. 48)

Soliciting Casework

So far, we have assumed that the level and growth of casework are determined by the demands of constituents, and in the process we may have commiserated a bit with the poor congressional offices inundated with requests for special service. Both our assumption and sympathy require some tempering. Despite bad-mouthing of the burden of casework mail, congressional offices perceive its political and humanitarian utility and would panic if it stopped coming. Additionally, most offices (86 percent in one study) actively go out and solicit cases (Johannes 1981, p. 538). It has become the standard for a member to encourage constituents to "bring your problems to me" in every speech and newsletter. One member puts up billboards with his picture, address, and the phrase "Can I Help?" (Yiannakis 1981, p. 570). Another Member uses his free telephone line to call constituents at random, asking, "Is there anything we can do for you?" (Yiannakis 1979, p. 523). Other members advertise their willingness to seek out grants by visiting with local leaders and giving them check-off "shopping lists" of government programs the leaders might like to be a part of. While the techniques vary, what comes into a congressional office often reflects what goes out. If the message is "here I am ready to do your errands," those kinds of requests will come in. Offices find a dramatic increase in casework requests after the Member has been back in the district or after sending out a newsletter offering help.

THE CONGRESSIONAL REACTION

The Motivation to Serve

Attention to casework is one of those areas where perceived self-interest and public interest converge to heighten casework's importance well beyond what is necessary. Members of Congress perceive their constituents as considerably more interested in casework than they actually are (see Table 3.1) and assume that effective constituency service is the key to reelection. But serving constituents' needs is regarded as more than simple political astuteness. Most legislators are interested in the well-being of constituents in their district and take pleasure in helping them challenge the monolithic bureaucracy (Breslin 1977, p. 19). Even a senator such as Alan Cranston (D-CA), known for his interest in legislation, asserts:

> Casework is the most critically important type of mail I receive. I believe the help I can give people in resolving their problems with government is a major responsibility of my office. (Cranston 1975, p. 17854)

In the words of a House member:

> Most people who write me have valid problems and feel that only their representatives can help them get action. Now sometimes they are wrong in sending things to us or in thinking their case has merit, but they are sincere, and I think it is one of the functions of a congressman to do what he can for them. (Olson 1966, p. 342)

Dealing with casework requires a commitment of resources. While this may mean the congressman's own time, most often it means staff effort. Only about one-third of House members report spending "a great deal of time on casework," with the average Member spending less than three hours per week (Johannes 1981, pp. 86–87). Analysis indicates that Democrats (Bond 1983, p. 18), and members from low-income districts commit more staff members to casework (Johannes and McAdams 1983, p. 9) than do their colleagues.

Senators, with their larger staffs and greater legislative responsibility, spend considerably less personal time on casework than do representatives. Based on the perceived electoral utility of casework, it comes as no surprise that junior and more politically insecure Members commit more personal and office resources to casework. For the junior member, casework may be a catharsis for frustration:

> A congressman lacking seniority, expertise and a network of relationships with other members may choose to throw his energies into the work of helping constituents; for here at least some results of his efforts are immediately apparent in contrast with his efforts in legislative work where he finds he has little influence. (Olson 1966, p. 342)

The emphasis junior Members give to casework also stems from the time period in which they entered politics.

> In an era of weakened parties and increasingly independent office-seekers, it is not surprising that successive classes of politicians adopt the latest "trendy" techniques of constituency relations—whether it is to impress constituents or to find an optimal means for blending their policy interests with a concern for efficient constituency service...new cohorts seem both to copy successful innovations and, at times, to do so with a vengeance (Johannes and McAdams 1983, p. 15)

Early commitment to casework by a significant number of congressmen is more than a passing phase worthy of mention but not concern:

> The emphasis freshman Members feel obliged to devote to service to constituents may have a formative effect on the concept of their roles. Through the process of active, daily involvement in the problems of individuals, they may be conditioned to view Congressional responsibilities in terms of particular, rather than general needs. (*Congressional Quarterly* 1976, p. 548)

While constituency service and legislative activity may not be mutually exclusive, they do compete for scarce resources. Thus emphasis on casework may well particularize politics and encourage members to ignore their legislative responsibilities.

The commitment to casework by U.S. legislators stands in sharp contrast to the norm in foreign legislatures:

> American congressmen, with their large personal staffs, are best equipped to perform such services; indeed, they solicit them by contact-

ing their constituents through newsletters, mass mailings, and radio broadcasts to make them aware of available services. European legislators lack the office facilities to run constituents' errands on the American scale. (Loewenberg and Patterson 1979, p. 188)

Casework Handling Routines

Who Handles the Cases?

The growth of casework accompanying the increased complexity of government has forced congressional offices to specialize in their handling of cases. Most offices employ staff members whose primary, if not exclusive, task involves dealing with individual cases. While virtually any staff member can deal with information requests, the knowledge and personal contacts necessary to unstick the bureaucracy requires motivation and experience. As David Mayhew (1974 p. 55) describes it, "Each office has skilled professionals who can play the bureaucracy like an organ—pushing the right pedals to produce desired effects."

Senate offices average three to five caseworkers, while some offices have ten (Breslin 1977, p. 22). House offices with their more limited staffs have fewer designated caseworkers, with a larger proportion of the staff doing casework along with its other duties (Johannes 1984, pp. 63–64). (See Figure 4.2.)

> Casework is handled rather routinely. The incoming constituent letter is judged for validity (there are a few, usually easy-to-spot, crank letters), and then assigned to a caseworker. Caseworkers are generally assigned certain subject areas and receive all letters within their specific areas. In this way, they gain expertise and develop contacts with agency personnel. (Carlile 1981, p. 18)

Increasingly, congressmen are handling casework from their district offices rather than from Washington. This makes a great deal of sense since it speeds communication and many cases end up getting handled by the regional offices of agencies (Fox and Hammond 1977, p. 77). This fact shows up in the dramatic increase in the number of district offices and the work patterns within them. While casework is the prime responsibility of only 12 percent of personal staffs in Washington, it is the main job of 49 percent of congressional district staffs (see Figure 4.2).

Case Handling Routines

Once they receive a request, caseworkers typically perform a cursory screening to determine whether the case has any merit. Merit is based on at least two criteria. Political merit stems from the nature of the con-

FIGURE 4.2

A COMPARISON OF HOUSE STAFF FUNCTIONS IN DISTRICT
AND WASHINGTON D.C. OFFICES
(percent of staff in each category)

WASHINGTON OFFICE STAFF		DISTRICT OFFICE STAFF	
		Legislative Research	1%
Communication: Press Work	8%	LEGISLATIVE MAIL	2%
		Personal Secretary	4%
Personal Secretary	10%	Communication: Press Work	10%
Office Supervision	11%	Office Supervision	15%
CASEWORK	12%	Clerical	18%
LEGISLATIVE MAIL	14%		
Clerical	18%	CASEWORK	49%
Legislative Research	23%		

SOURCE: U.S., Congress, House. Commission on Administrative Review 1977, pp.
1025-26.

stituent who is writing. Most offices will not consider cases from individuals outside their constituency, preferring to pass on the additional
workload to another office with a "buck" slip. An exception to this pattern occurs after redistricting, when a Member gaining new territory often begins to service its needs. While congressional offices argue that this
facilitates the orderly transfer of casework to the new constituency, the
potential political payoffs for a Member in need of solidifying his political base in new territory does not reduce the motivation to serve (Yadlosky and Bird 1981, p. 1499). While offices argue that casework is non-
partisan and nondiscriminatory, there is "always an inclination to give
special service to those most influential state constituents" (Breslin 1977,
p. 31). Not only are the kinds of people who write for help more
representative of the active and attentive segments of the constituency
(Mayhew 1974, p. 109), but those activists known to a congressional office will see their cases brought to the top of the pile.

Substantive merit is much harder to judge. Outrageous requests or a situation where the constituent has not taken even the first simple step to solve the problem will generally be turned back with a polite response explaining the office's inability to handle the case (and an invitation to "call on us again if you have further problems"), or with a suggestion that the constituent should try contacting the office in question first and if not satisfied write again (see Chapter 7 for examples of unreasonable requests). Generally congressional offices will not handle cases where a lawyer is involved, preferring to let the lawyer earn his fee. Some constituents have caught on to this. When Senator Pete Domenici (D–NM) asked a constituent why he had come to him for help in retrieving his car (which was being held for delinquent taxes) rather than going to a lawyer, the constituent answered, "I'd have to pay a lawyer. You can do it for me free" (Johnson 1981). In assessing merit, caseworkers look for different interpretations of the law, inordinate delays in handling problems, and mitigating circumstances crying out for exceptions to the letter of the law. If anything, congressional offices err on the side of taking on more questionable cases than justified. As one congressman explained it, "Undeserving or not, a request to my office is going to be passed on. It's necessary for me, as a matter of public relations" (Gellhorn 1966, p. 69). Most Members argue that they are not asking for anything which the constituent does not deserve and that their involvement just hastens the solving of the problem.

Once deciding to take on a case, the caseworker drafts a letter of acknowledgement to the constituent pledging to contact the appropriate office and keep him appraised of developments. The caseworker will then attach a "buck slip" to a copy of the original letter and send it to the appropriate bureaucratic office for response. The experienced caseworkers with well-developed contacts in various agencies will often call their contacts to warn them of an impending case arrival and thereby highlight the case's importance (see Westin 1973, pp. 60–65).

Fearing that even a congressional request might get lost in the bureaucratic labyrinth, caseworkers generally develop either a manual "cases pending" file, which they check on a regular basis, or a computerized "tickler" system (Jost 1979, p. 50), reminding them to follow up on open cases.

THE BUREAUCRATIC RESPONSE

The Motivation to Respond

While few observers would argue that bureaucrats intentionally thwart the interests of citizens, the volume of decisions and the anonymity of individuals involved allow bureaucrats to take refuge in compulsive attachment to formal rules and procedures in the name of fairness and justice (see Matthews 1960, p. 225). The involvement of a congressional office in a particular case may strike the bureaucrat as pleading for a narrow special case, but it changes effectively the terrain of battle. With the increased visibility, effective handling of a case becomes a criterion for judging the total bureaucracy in question. Through its control over budgets, reorganization, and program legislation, the Congress and its individual members stand out as players who should not be crossed by bureaucrats interested in the future well-being of their agencies:

> The agency's vested interest in Congressional favor, and the Senator's or Representative's vested interest in the constituent's favor, may be the most convincing guarantee that the bureaucracy will be attentive to individual citizens. (*Congressional Quarterly* 1976, p. 549)

Patterns of Response

Most governmental agencies have established legislative liaison offices to deal with congressional requests. Those agencies involved with numerous cases go to great effort in making responsiveness a goal. For example, each branch of the military maintains well-staffed contingents within the congressional office buildings to handle the thousands of requests received each week. The State Department maintains a 24-hour hotline to handle congressional requests to help constituents who have lost their passports overseas or who need a passport immediately in hardship cases.

At a minimum, congressional involvement in a case brings it to the front of the line (and thereby bypasses other citizens who followed procedures and dealt with the agency directly) and assures a quick, if not always desired, response:

> Every administrator moves fast when dealing with a congressman's case. . . . Some cases must be retarded when more favored ones are being pulled out for quick action. . . . Since slow administration begets many complaints, complainants on that score are presumably made happier (and therefore become grateful to congressmen) when slowness is overcome. (Gellhorn 1966, p. 77)

Agencies generally "pay more attention to citizens' complaints, however trivial, channeled through congressional offices, than to serious problems brought directly to the attention of administrators" (Johannes

1981, p. 91). As Morris Ogul points out (1976 p. 172), the bureaucracy works on the "squeaky wheel gets the grease" principle. And congressional offices can make a louder "squeak" than individuals or other units of government.

From one agency to the next, the story is the same. Deputy Postmaster General Fred Belen asserted, "I read every congressional letter" (Ogul 1976, p. 172). In the Veterans' Administration, a simple inquiry from a congressional office assures a high-level Washington review (Gellhorn 1966, p. 68). When the Offices of Legislative Affairs of the military are asked by a congressional office to hop, they ask "how high?" Some agencies are more dependent on direct congressional goodwill, since they have few citizen advocates touting their utility and effectiveness:

> Especially in agencies such as the Department of State that have little or no public constituency, there is a strong desire to be as responsive as possible to congressional case referrals. State, for example, places high priority on such responses; in its corridors, one often sees a young Foreign Service officer hurrying by with a large, bluebordered file marked "Congressional" to seek clearances from the bureaus concerned. Part of the emphasis placed on handling congressional inquiries in State comes from the (possibly mistaken) assumption that "the more satisfactorily it handles constituent-initiated requests, the more likely it is to obtain the support of members [of Congress] on policy." (Dodd and Schott 1979, p. 268)

Casework Success

Determining the utility of congressional intervention is difficult. Estimates of securing an outcome favorable for the constituents vary from 10 percent to 40 percent (see Gellhorn 1966, p. 79; Clapp 1963, p. 78; Johannes and McAdams 1981, p. 534; Carlile 1981a, p. 19). There is some evidence that levels of success have gone up in recent years, which may reflect increased caseworker skill and effort (Carlile 1981a, p. 19). Empirical measurements of case success may not be completely straightforward. Former Congressman Page Belcher (R–OK) tells the story of a military hardship case from a wife who wanted to get her husband out of the army. After considerable effort the task was completed and the results were communicated with pleasure. The next week's mail contained a new case request from the husband who wanted the decision reversed because he had joined the Army to get away from his wife.

Despite the extraordinary responsiveness of U.S. congressmen, citizen expectations may outstrip realistic possibilities. This can often be true with immigration cases.

Many constituents come from governments with unapproachable officials. Once in the United States, these constituents are shocked at what seems indifferent treatment in this land of equality. On the other hand, having grown up under a system where help was based on bribes and contacts, the alien finds it unbelievable that no matter whom he knows, he must wait his turn for action. (*Congressional Staff Journal* 1982a, p. 10)

Variation in success rates across congressional offices depends on both who you are and what you do. Members of committees with oversight responsibilities for specific agencies have a more direct conduit to immediate and favorable response from that agency than do other members. Realizing this natural tendency to keep in the good graces of those holding the most proximate control, some congressmen seek out positions on committees and subcommittees having oversight over agencies of a particular concern to their constituents. At times a Member of the "right" committee can bend administrative decision considerably:

We recently told a representative that we wanted to be friends, and if he insisted upon a decision we thought was a bit over the line, we would give it to him. But we also said that we had only a very few blue chips to play with in this game. He could have one of them if he wanted it, but we hoped he would remember where it came from and would realize there weren't many more we could hand over if he needed one badly in the future. (legislative liaison official, quoted in Gellhorn 1966, p. 72)

While variations in success of different offices are evident, Johannes's comprehensive study concludes that casework success is "less a matter of clout than of diligence, caseworker skills, the inherent merit of cases and clear communications" (Johannes 1984, pp. 146–47).

The effort put into casework varies from one office and one case to the next. Well-trained and experienced caseworkers are likely to have the important personal contacts which can unstick the most intransigent bureaucracy. Skillful caseworkers know how to communicate their level of interest both in what they say and how they say it:

Sometimes we think that they [administrators] must all be sent to school where they teach them that if a senator's office sends over a case with a "buck slip" they can safely forget it; if the request is contained in a letter from the senator, this demands more attention: if there is a call from the senator's staff, it's still more important; and if the senator calls himself, do it. (Matthews 1960, p. 227)

While it is not unheard of for a congressman to take personal action on a pending case, it is rare, and thus carries considerable weight. A congressman who gets personally involved too often with an agency to emphasize the "unique and earth-shattering importance" of too many cases becomes viewed like the child who cried wolf, and the effectiveness of that tactic is diminished for him.

THE CONGRESSIONAL OFFICE RESPONSE

Once the congressional office hears the agency's response to a particular case, it structures its response to the constituent to get the maximum credit and avoid even minimum blame. If the decision is favorable, the office takes full responsibility to contact the constituent with the good news, paraphrasing the agency response or perhaps even calling the constituent directly to "share in his or her joy." If the decision is unfavorable, responses are structured so that the agency takes the blame. The agency often writes the letter, referring to the efforts of the congressional office, but pointing out that despite its efforts a negative decision resulted. The congressional office often sends a follow-up letter commiserating with the constituent in his or her battle against the "huge and faceless bureaucracy" and urging the constituent to contact the office again if further problems arise.

CITIZEN SATISFACTION

Although less than half the cases result in changed bureaucratic decisions, recent surveys show that over two-thirds of the citizens requesting help from their congressmen are "very satisfied" with the results and feel that the congressional office had "done its very best" to solve their problem (see Cavanaugh 1979, p. 228 and Fiorina 1981, p. 535).

For the congressional office, the act of intervention may be just as important as objective success or failure. As one member of Congress put it:

> We get forty requests a week for help. Half of them we can't do anything about. Some we can. But they all get a sympathetic ear. That's what people want more than anything else, a sympathetic ear. (Fenno 1978, p. 108)

THE POLITICAL IMPLICATIONS OF CASEWORK

Perceptions of Importance

The conventional wisdom is virtually unanimous that casework has direct electoral benefits for members of Congress. In a series of surveys,

82 percent of House members and over 86 percent of the staff felt that constituents receiving help would vote for the Member taking up their cause (Johannes and McAdams 1981, p. 517; Fiorina 1981, p. 545). As the following quotes reflect, observers of the casework process see it as a quid pro quo situation where voters exchange their support for congressional consideration of their special problems:

> Casework is undoubtedly an important Congressional function. In encouraging constituents to take advantage of their service, many Members are acting on the supposition that a satisfied constituent is a vote gained in the next election; the corollary is that a dissatisfied constituent may well be a vote irretrievably lost. (Carlile 1981, p. 21)

> To many voters the incumbent's district office operations and personal record of service may appear to be largely a reflection of his personal efforts, and therefore contingent on his re-election. If these voters opt for the material and instrumental over the symbolic, does this make them irrational? If so, classical political machines are based on irrationality. (Fiorina 1981, p. 565)

> The allocation of resources to constituency services is not only a good but a necessary investment for members. The odds are strong that taking on a case will result in a more favorable impression of the member. (Cavanaugh 1979, p. 241)

> Voters, essentially, are ingrates. Casework fails to produce a significant effect on the vote because constituents fully expect their congressmen to render such personal "bureaucratic unsticking services" for them. (Johannes and McAdams 1981, p. 537)

The positive impact of casework is not perceived as being limited to increased support by the affected citizen. Citizens tell their family and friends about positive interactions with their congressman, and a positive reputation for "helping the folks back home" gains political benefits even from individuals never feeling the need to pursue help.

The Actual Impact of Casework

Seldom is the conventional wisdom about a political phenomenon so strong and the empirical verification so lacking. While asserting that service opportunities give congressmen the chance to improve their support by three to five percent (Fiorina 1977, p. 53), the empirical evidence is inconsistent. Members committing more resources and performing more casework fail to increase their vote totals more than less aggressive Members (Johannes and McAdams 1981, p. 530; Johannes 1984, pp.

187–211). A number of factors stand out as possible explanations for this lack of empirical verification. In the first place, casework directly affects only about 15 percent of constituents (Davidson and Oleszek 1981, p. 121), and a relatively large proportion of citizens getting help do not vote (Johannes and McAdams 1981, p. 531). Thus the impact of casework recipients is diluted by the total constituency. Additionally, in committing resources to casework effort, members are often anticipating future political difficulty or reacting to past weaknesses. With many of the most politically weak members jumping on the constituency service bandwagon, it would not be surprising that a clear cause and effect relationship does not appear in the empirical evidence. Finally, politicians tend to be strategically conservative. Members not only redouble their casework efforts to strengthen their political base, but congressmen with a strong base may attribute it to their past efforts in serving constituents and maintain an established pattern well after it has lost its utility.

Whatever the case, congressmen and their staffs act as if casework has a political payoff.

THE IMPLICATIONS OF CASEWORK FOR THE POLITICAL SYSTEM AND FOR CONGRESS AS AN INSTITUTION

Supposed Advantages of Casework

Solving Problems

Whatever is said about the general impact of casework, it does solve specific problems for some individuals for whom that problem is the most vital aspect of their interaction with government at that particular time. Life is made up of little skirmishes rather than life-long battles, and any process which contributes to justice prevailing in one of the skirmishes serves a purpose. Constituents delayed or shunted aside by a bureaucracy blinded by a slavish commitment to the rules or made insensitive by lack of contact with the human beings affected by their administrative decision need a powerful champion:

> The congressional recourse is there for anyone who is aware of it and wants to use it. It may provide a way of registering need intensity not available through administrative channels. Moreover, in an age of proliferating bureaucracies it would be foolish to derogate any governmental process that offers individual attention. (Mayhew 1974, p. 109)

Members of Congress are uniquely accessible to even the least powerful individual:

From the Congress, and more particularly from the idea of homestate congressmen, these men derive a sense of protection, of a friend in power, of an accessible person who is not likely to be protected by a number of secretaries. The right of petition here is expressed in personal, human contact, not through paper forms and proper channels. (Lane 1962, p. 66)

Freeing Decision-Makers

For the individual congressman, a successful constituency service operation not only provides satisfaction through concrete examples of success, but may relieve him of some of the political concerns and allow him to perform his legislative task more effectively:

Many Senators have commented that they are able to take controversial positions only because they have built up a solid reputation for constituent service. This tends to provide a reservoir of good will that the Senator can rely upon in times of political controversy. (Breslin 1982, p. 29)

Enhancing Bureaucratic Oversight

The most positive claim concerning legislative casework asserts that the existence of casework improves Congress's ability to oversee the administration of the laws it passes. Oversight purportedly has two benefits. First of all, the fact that even the most routine bureaucratic decision can be called into question provides a threat which "helps insure that the federal bureaucracy will anticipate problems before they arise and will not neglect its duties" (Olson 1966, p. 339).

Secondly, bringing casework problems to the attention of congressmen sets the stage for corrective legislation:

The first and most indirect consequence of casework for oversight was that members gained some appreciation of, and information about, certain bureaucratic operations. . . . Beyond gaining a general sense of operations and general information, congressmen became aware of certain deficiencies in policy implementation. . . the progression from casework to awareness of problems to action was a standard subpattern in congressional behavior. Heightened awareness of possible bureaucratic error was no guarantee that members of Congress would do anything about the situation, but action was more likely once such awareness did develop. (Ogul 1976, pp. 166–67)

Congressmen report many pieces of legislation stemming from single constituent complaints, such as excluding certain reimbursed moving expenses from income, establishing a small tax division within the Tax Court, exempting certain individuals from the draft, and changing the payment procedures for Medicare (see Ogul 1976, p. 170 and Fox and Hammond 1977, p. 91). While these examples do not exhibit the characteristics of earth-shattering policy initiatives, they were important to the individual constituents suggesting them and to other citizens in a similar situation.

While there are numerous examples of casework triggering improved administration by the bureaucracy or corrective legislation, they are the exception rather than the rule. Most of the casework referrals fail to spur agencies to increase their general effectiveness or fairness but rather are "handled at the same level of the agency (often by the same official) where the complaint arose in the first place" (Dodd and Schott 1979, p. 270). Individual bureaucrats handling hundreds of decisions each year generally have so few of them questioned that the remote threat of congressional intervention means relatively little. Although some argue that casework should lead to corrective legislation, the decentralized nature of casework being handled on an office-by-office basis, the fact that less than one-third of the offices keep any record on casework load and recurring problems (Ogul 1976, p. 165), and the lack of congressional motivation to generalize from specific cases mitigate against general policy emanating from cases. The legislative side of a congressman's staff either may not be aware of ineffective legislation or administration, or a spate of similar problems may be explained by unique characteristics of the district rather than seen as a general problem deserving investigation. From a motivation perspective,

> the chief drawback to using casework as a strong device for monitoring executive agencies involves the motivations of the individual members. Casework is important because it is vital to the image of the member—that he or she is responding to constituents, getting something done...getting the case processed is more important than the use of a number of cases in developing a pattern of agency performance or lack thereof. What oversight does result is often a kind of by-product rather than a calculated effort. (Dodd and Schott 1979, p. 271)

Thus, while casework is not contradictory to the goal of improving Congress as an oversight body, the way in which casework is viewed and handled limits its contribution.

The Disadvantages of Casework

The Impact on the Congressman

One of the scarcest resources for a member of Congress is personal and staff time to meet the many facets of the job. Casework consumes the vast majority of congressional staff time and effort, and a significant portion of many congressmen's efforts. Roger Davidson (Davidson and Oleszek 1981, p. 9) outlines the "two Congresses" as the classic dilemma faced by a congressman. The Congress seen from the outside places heavy demands on the Member to satisfy constituents and bolster re-election chances. The inside Congress demands policy innovation, policy coordination, and the Member's personal desire to prove himself to his colleagues and enhance personal power. Resources given over to case-work mean fewer resources for the other facets of the legislative role, par-ticularly legislative tasks. The impact of this imbalance may go well be-yond the individual Members and their contributions to legislation:

> It is easy to dismiss constituency service activities as too trivial or de-meaning for the Congress to engage in. But to the extent that they satisfy the legitimate needs and desires of constituents, they serve a pur-pose of quite literally bringing government closer to the people. It is the tradeoffs they engender that are a source of strain for congressional per-formance. Member inattention to pending bills today means poor legis-lation, and poor implementation tomorrow...and increased casework is the result, which in turn aggravates the existing misallocation of mem-ber time and staff. (Cavanaugh 1981, p. 75)

Dealing with casework is not a finite demand on one's time which with a bit of effort will solve the problem once and for all. Developing a reputation for effective casework creates increased expectations and in-creased demands. By making intervention in the bureaucracy look easy (and thus verifying the Member's "clout" in Washington for his consti-tuents), the congressman unleashes a double burden. Constituents over-estimate their congressmen's range and degree of effectiveness, and the congressmen must redouble their efforts just to stand still in constituents' esteem. The once-appreciated becomes commonplace, and appreciation turns into "what have you done for me lately?"

Emphasis on casework can become a refuge for Members unwilling to face up to the conflict involved in policymaking. Taking stands on im-portant policies can make as many enemies as friends, while casework largely breeds friends and supporters (Fiorina 1977, p. 46).

While it is impossible empirically to prove the direct impact of case-work on electoral security, the ability to take credit for constituency serv-ice clearly is one of the contributing factors to incumbent security in Con-gress. There may be nothing inherently wrong with the vast majority (over 90 percent in the House and 80 percent in the Senate) of incum-bents winning reelection; nevertheless, the situation where they tend to win in spite of rather than because of their positions on public issues shakes the foundation of representation and responsiveness. Effective in-cumbent casework often insulates the incumbent from a meaningful electoral challenge where the full range of his performance would be on the line (Johannes 1981, p. 85).

While it has become expected that congressmen will willingly seek to serve the personal casework interests of their constituents, some voices of concern and dissent are beginning to emerge. One congressman complained:

> I thought I was going to be Daniel Webster and I found that most of my work consisted of personal work for constituents. . . . This life consists of preoccupation with the unimportant at the expense of the more important. . . . The least appealing aspect of my job is the service we have to perform for constituents. (Clapp 1963, pp. 51-55)

Others described casework as "trivial, onerous and burdensome" (Ogul 1976, p. 162). The burdensome demands of casework were specified as one of the top two problems members of the House outlined as thwarting Congress in its job (U.S., Congress, House. Commission on Administrative Review 1977, pp. 868-69). Over 50 percent of the congressional respondents specifically indicated that constituency work interfered with their legislative tasks (Ibid. pp. 875-76). Former Senator Fulbright (D-AK) summed up the frustration and its broader ramifications:

> Power, unlike money, is a wasting asset. . . it must be used or it does not exist. Real power is the bringing to bear of significant influence on the course of human events. An office holder whose career is devoted to ombudsman service—useful though this might be—. . . will find at the end of his career, if he stops to think of it, that he never wielded power at all. (Fulbright 1979, p. 730)

The emphasis on casework can also reorient a congressman's entire view of the political process. Preoccupation with narrow problems and anomolies discourages concern over long-term solutions to problems. Emphasis on the symptoms rather than the causes of problems retards solving problems once and for all. As Richard Fenno (Ranney 1981, p. 73) observes, casework leads congressmen to become "inductive" thinkers focusing on narrow problems, rather than "deductive" analysts working toward general solutions.

The Impact on the Bureaucracy

The intermittent interjection of congressional concern into administration may stir bureaucrats to better performance, but it also "prevents suitable emphasis on getting the job done correctly in the first place" (Gellhorn 1976, p. 81). Bureaucrats, congressmen, and citizens alike take false solace in the fact that congressional intervention is always available to solve the most onerous mistakes, while the routine "garden variety" mistakes continue.

The Impact on Citizens

For every citizen who is helped by casework, thousands of other worthy cases never reach the congressional office. Some constituents bring worthy cases to congressional offices with limited interest, skill, or clout for handling them and thus get less service than other citizens. As former Senator William Fulbright (D–AK) complains:

> The modern legislator, with some admirable exceptions, has discarded the role of educator in favor of performing services for his constituents— and not really his constituents as a community, but the best organized, best funded, and most politically active interest groups within the constituency. (Fulbright 1979, p. 723)

Furthermore, successful shortcutting of the administrative process by a congressional office places one citizen's case at the head of the line, while the less aggressive or aware citizen who followed normal channels has his case retarded.

> The artificially high priority accorded congressional. . . mail slows other business. Those aggrieved may then write the President or a Congressman to complain about delays in matters of interest to complainants— thus the wheel is given another spin. Since a communication's importance seems to be appraised more by its source than its content, the picayune often takes precedence over the profound. (Dodd and Schott 1979, p. 269)

The evaluation of casework is not black-and-white. No one wants to throw the baby out with the bathwater. Every observer agrees that there is a significant number of situations where congressional intervention in the bureaucracy is warranted and useful. The prime frustrations are (1) that casework has not lived up to its potential for ameliorating injustice with equality and fairness, or for improving legislation and administration in general and (2) that casework takes up an inordinate amount of congressional effort with little benefit outside of solving a relatively few isolated problems and securing the electoral base of incumbent legislators.

The Impact on Political Choice

The opportunity to serve constituents through casework creates a sense of satisfaction and indebtedness which increases incumbent's chances for reelection. While the extraordinary reelection rates of congressional incumbents assures a legislature staffed with experienced Members, it can also lead to stagnation. Challengers hesitate to confront Members with good casework records, and election campaigns are often devoid of issue considerations.

Congressman Ron Paul (R-TX) goes a step further in condemning the incumbent advantages of casework:

> Congressmen should not be elected just to end up as errand boys. It's a moral as well as a political problem. If I used my money to bribe people, we all know that would be illegal and corrupt. But if I rob the national treasure because of political chicanery—just to get re-elected—then Congress becomes a legal way to help your own political cause.(Johnson 1981)

SOME PROPOSALS FOR CHANGE

Proponents of casework reform start with the assumption that congressmen will continue to play an integral part in the process of satisfying constituent problems with the bureaucracy. Proposals to establish an independent "ombudsman" system such as that used in some Scandinavian countries receive little support from those who recognize the political benefits members now receive from casework. Over the years Congressman Henry Reuss (D-WI) has proposed creating an Office of Administrative Counsel which supposedly would increase efficiency and reduce the workload of individual congressional offices by allowing offices to refer their cases to a central office with a better-trained staff who, because of the volume, would create more effective ways to get bureaucratic response. Centralization would also facilitate the oversight function by accumulating congress-wide statistics on administrative trouble spots. Cognizant of political considerations, The Office of Administrative Counsel would only take cases on referral from congressional offices and would allow offices to announce and take credit for success and put blame back on itself (Gellhorn 1966, p. 88). While looking logical on the surface, the Administrative Counsel proposal lies dormant in the legislative process, with Members fearful that their credit claiming could suffer and that they may just be creating another big bureaucracy between themselves and the agencies. On a much more limited level, some congressional offices have joined forces to hire caseworkers, share information, and increase their individual clout. A prime example is the joint district offices established by Senators Lugar and Quale (R-IN):

> The casework in general is handled jointly. Letters from constituents sent separately to both Senators go in one file; the matter is handled

by a combined caseworker; and outgoing correspondence bears both Senators' names. Letters about casework which are addressed to only one Senator receive the same joint treatment unless they involve "very personal matters or exceptional situations...or unless it is clear that the writer is a close, personal friend of the Senator to whom he wrote."...The handling of casework on a combined basis saves time, money and duplication. (*Congressional Staff Journal*, 1982, p. 6)

Despite the obvious advantage of such an approach, it was possible only after settling particular credit claiming concerns such as whose name would come first when the phone was answered (they alternate months). Such cooperation would probably not have been possible if both senators were not from the same party and did not share basic positions on public issues.

In general though, the handling of casework is done today in about the same way as a century ago. The volume is larger, the variety greater, and the pressure to perform enhanced, but the procedures vary little. For those citizens who know how to use the system, casework can ameliorate many of the frustrations of dealing with the bureaucracy in this bureaucratic age. The congressmen, as long as most of the work can be handled by staff and their freedom is not seriously challenged, will hang on to a system which gives them many political benefits with few obvious costs.

CHAPTER 5

THE BURDEN AND OPPORTUNITY OF ISSUE MAIL

On several occasions I can testify that a single thoughtful, factually persuasive letter did change my mind or cause me to initiate a review of a previous judgment. (Congressman Morris Udall, quoted in *Congressional Quarterly* 1976, p. 547)

On the whole, mail is more trouble than it is worth as a reflection of public opinion. Public sentiment can be more accurately checked by reading the newspapers, talking to or corresponding with political and leadership groups and conducting or following public opinion polls. (Former Senator Joseph Clark 1964, p. 61)

Writing your congressman can have an impact. It is true that most letters from constituents never reach the congressman's desk, but they all reach his office. Although most mail gets little more than a glance from a busy clerk, there are letters that electrify, that counter false information, that change votes. (Green 1979, p. 307)

As the above quotes indicate, the expectations and perceptions concerning the impact of constituents' communications on the policymaking process vary dramatically. Part of the disagreement stems from an idealized picture of democracy whose unrealistic expectations raise hopes too high. Believing in James Madison's criterion for democracy that Congress "should have an immediate dependence on and an intimate sympathy with the people" (*Federalist #35*) does not necessarily mean that representative government fails unless the vast majority of citizens stands over the shoulders of their legislators giving advice and suggestions on every decision. In a complex society where politics is only one of a citizen's many concerns, we should not be surprised that the average constituent only infrequently has his concern agitated enough to respond. The question is not whether citizens affect every decision, but whether they can affect the outcome in enough cases to make their concern a threat.

While this analysis may not be able to answer this question once and for all, some clear clues indicate that legislative mail is important. In the first place, constituents believe that writing their congressmen is worthwhile and increasingly take the effort to communicate. The effort congressional offices make in counting, analyzing, and responding to issue mail signals their evaluation of its importance. In analyzing congressional voting decisions, John Kingdon (1981, p. 55) found that over one-quarter of the congressmen spontaneously mentioned constituent mail as an important factor in their decisions on a wide variety of issues. The impact of constituent mail has been verified by a number of cases where one letter changed legislative history, or a flood of letters assured victory or defeat of proposed legislation. From the perspectives of the participants, the general conclusion is that constituent mail can count.

THE NATURE OF INCOMING ISSUE MAIL

Issue mail includes those letters, postcards, and telegrams which go beyond asking for information or seeking out the congressman's views and either explicitly or implicitly express an opinion on issues of public policy in the hopes of influencing the member of Congress. The message is more than an abstract "be responsive," but is rather "be responsive to me on this particular issue."

Issue mail falls into three basic categories: individual "cold sweat" communications, inspired mail, and constituent poll responses. "Cold sweat" letters are those from individual constituents who wake up in a cold sweat in the middle of the night with a burning concern over a nagging problem or pending policy decision. In most cases, the issue has a direct impact on the writer's individual well-being, although interests "need not be selfish, [and] can be altruistic" (Pitkin and Shumer 1982, p. 48). More people, though, tend to write out of fear than out of hope. Nothing spurs individual writers more than the fear of losing something government provides or protects. Once a constituent has become used to a particular benefit, his desire to keep it far outstrips the willingness of a fellow citizen to work for a new benefit he has not become accustomed to. There is little evidence that individually motivated letters have become dramatically more frequent in recent years. Their volume seems to vary with the nature and public awareness of particular issues. When policy initiatives involve cutting back on government activities, as under President Reagan's budget plans, we would expect a public out-cry from those citizens whose pet programs are being cut.

The "growth stock" in constituent communications is "inspired mail," those communications planned, instigated, and facilitated by or-ganized interest groups. Realizing the impact of constituent letters, in-terest groups of every stripe use a wide variety of tactics to get their members to write their congressmen. As TEXPAC, the political action committee of the Texas Medical Association, tells its members, "The voice of one whispers. . . . A voice of many influences" (Anderson 1983, p. 33). In some cases, the process is a one-shot attempt to promote or change a specific decision. In 1982, when Congress supported President Reagan's plan to withhold taxes on interest and dividends, the banking industry pulled out all the stops to get the plan repealed. Full page ads in major newpapers, letters to depositors, and the provision of free speakers to business and senior citizen groups advertised the issue. Mail-back postcards were provided to customers at teller windows and in monthly statements. The campaign produced an estimated 22 million let-ters and postcards to flood Capitol Hill (Edsall 1983, p. al). In a dramatic reversal of a decision made less than a year before, the repeal passed in the House 382 to 41 and in the Senate 91 to 5. Supporters of the repeal drive, such as Congressman Norman D'Amours (D–NH), hailed the con-stituent outpouring and congressional reaction as "democracy in ac-tion. . . the voice of the people [being] heard" (quoted in ibid.). On the other hand, opponents such as Congressman Robert Matsui (D–CA) and Barber Conable Jr. (R–NY) characterized it as "undemocratic" and "a freight train coming down the track" (Ibid.).

Interest groups contemplating mass-mail campaigns have become more sophisticated in motivating citizens and increasing the possible im-pact of their communications. The first rule for an effective campaign is to make it easy for the citizens. Providing free postage of preprinted cards or letters will get more action from constituents than requiring the extra effort of having the person write an original letter. Unfortunately, such low-effort responses are easy to spot, so some groups go to a great deal of effort to mislead the congressional offices by printing letters on different types of paper and imprinting them with the writer's name and address to look like personal stationery (Keller 1982).

Groups involved in longer-term campaigns or desiring an impact on a wide variety of issues go even further to increase chances of success. Organizations with as widely varying goals as Common Cause, the Na-tional Rifle Association, and The American Association of University Professors have organized their membership lists by congressional dis-trict, which allows them to send out "legislative alerts" to specific Mem-bers or kinds of Members. Some campaigns may focus on Members of particular committees, while others focus on Members with weak electoral margins. Realizing that time is important, some groups go a step further and get prior permission to produce letters over individuals' signatures at the appropriate time:

> Even with the speediest presses, producing a mass mailing and getting it returned back to Congress can take weeks. The mail may hit Capitol Hill too early or too late to help. Some interest groups have solved that problem by collecting proxies of their supporters in advance...the NEA (National Education Association) has collected permission from 100,000 teachers to sign their names to telegrams on issues ranging from tuition tax credits to Social Security. The telegrams pour in when they are needed. (Keller 1982)

With the effectiveness of computerized mailing techniques, it is no longer necessary to have groups of organized and motivated individuals in order to bombard Congress with mail. By purchasing mailing lists of people likely to support your cause, it is possible to create a powerful issue constituency out of whole cloth. Through successive testing of various mailing lists for willingness to respond, relatively heterogeneous "first generation" mailing lists can be pared down to a group of rabid activists with the will to write high-effort personal letters on specific issues.

Inspired mail brings into a congressional office a great volume of mail from a wide range of constituents. While on the surface this would seemingly provide congressmen with more insight into constituent views, some problems are evident. Only certain kinds of issues and positions on those issues are likely to have an adequately resourceful organization out there to inspire communications. The kinds of people in the communications network (on mailing lists and in organizations) and those who bother to respond are clearly not a random sample of the population. Additionally, constituents who write only because they are pressured or who have to have their hands held through the whole process may really have little basic interest in the issue at hand. After receiving a large volume of mail on an issue,

> one Representative telephoned a random selection of his correspondents to test their knowledge of labor legislation they had written about. He found that they had written because they had been told to or because they had gotten excited; they did not know the issues, could not specify what they disliked in the committee bill, and could not compare the competing bills. (*Congressional Quarterly* 1976, p. 534)

As we will see later, the intelligent member of Congress takes these limitations into account when evaluating mail that seems to have been inspired by an outside source.

A third kind of issue mail involves responses to constituent polls sent out by congressional offices. The once unique (Wilcox 1966, p. 527) procedure of sending out constituent polls on a regular basis has become a common tactic for congressional offices. While congressmen often express how impressed they are "by the enthusiasm with which my constituents took part in this survey" (Udall 1964, p. 22446), congressional polls have too many impediments to be viewed as true representations of constituent views.

Most constituent polls include basic methodological flaws which mean that their results are hardly worth the paper they are written on. Few congressional staff members have the skills to develop a polling technique which is completely neutral and statistically reliable. Good polls include only neutral questions which do not lead the respondent to a particular response through wording, prestige endorsements, or available options. The language of some congressional poll questions almost predetermines the response (see Chapter 6 for a more detailed discussion). Not only do the questions often seem faulty, but the volume and nature of respondents casts a dark pall on the results. With voluntary responses requiring the constituent to take some effort in filling out the poll and paying for its return, only a certain segment of any constituency will make the attempt. While Congressman Morris Udall typically applauded the "enthusiasm" of his constituents and took four pages of the *Congressional Record* to describe his poll results (Udall 1964, p. 22446), his equally typical nine percent response rate brings the results into severe question.

Few congressmen have much faith in polls as good measures of constituent opinion. Less than one percent of the congressmen surveyed by the House Commission on Administrative Review mentioned constituent polls as useful sources of information for making policy decisions (U.S., Congress, House, Commission on Administrative Review 1977, p. 967). Despite the awareness of their methodological shortcomings and limited informational utility, the constituent polls have become a well-established tradition. To understand this seeming irrationality one must only realize that the form is more important than the substance. The sending out of a poll is a low-cost way of communicating to constituents that the congressman cares about district attitudes, whether or not the poll helps him measure them. Biased questions may in fact help the congressman verify that he is in tune with his constituents by shoving the results right back in the face of those who disagree with him. Some Members brandish sheaves of poll results on the floor and quote from them extensively to justify votes, thereby insulating themselves from future criticisms and helping solidify an image of responsiveness.

METHODS OF HANDLING THE ISSUE MAIL

Issue mail, especially when it comes at the volition of an individual constituent, is both a special burden and opportunity for the congressional office. As an opportunity, a letter from a concerned constituent gives the congressman a rare look at that factor which just may be the key to that constituent's vote. In most congressional offices, the first step in handling an issue letter is to immediately put that voter on a mailing list of like-minded individuals who have already written with similar views on that issue. Once on this list, the constituent is in line for future unsolicited communications giving him updates on the issue and for often laudatory epistles highlighting the congressman's unending efforts to solve the problem.

On the burden side, most congressmen believe that "constituents who are deeply concerned and write thoughtful, reasoned letters deserve appropriately responsive answers" (Tacheron and Udall 1970, p. 81). Framing responses which will satisfy the individual constituent and not cause political damage among the broader constituency (and, of course, hopefully have a broad positive effect) is a tremendous challenge. Constituents who write are often very specific about the kind of policy they want and have little understanding or patience for a decision-making system which works slowly and on the basis of compromise and bargaining.

Form Letters Versus Original Compositions

Congressional offices realize intimately the tension between wanting to be personally responsive to individual constituents by writing original letters to each correspondent and the realities of finite time resources and large volumes of mail. In most cases contemporary congressional offices write original letters to constituents corresponding to issues which generate few letters and rely on form letters where it is economical to handle many letters on the same issue. Increasingly, congressional offices are using the computer to get the best of both worlds. The computer allows a staff member to choose from a set of prewritten paragraphs and "compose" a letter which faces up to each of the issues and its various nuances for each constituent. Sophisticated typewriters with the "IBM Selectric" look and autopens which copy a Member's signature make it difficult for even the most sophisticated constituent to realize that the letter was not originally written for them. Some offices go so far as to look for clues such as informality in the salutation or signature and repeat this in the letter to imply personalization.

For constituents who hold on to the archaic notion that their congressman is going to read every letter and agonize over writing a personal response, such impersonalization seems like trickery. But once one realizes that the mail workload (not to mention increasing legislative demands in other realms) makes this image unrealistic, attempts at increasing efficiency are less threatening. Since everything coming out of a congressional office can reflect positively or negatively on the Member, few congressmen allow their mail-handling procedures to go on without oversight. Staff work closely with the Member, developing standard replies reflecting the Member's views and going over strategies for responding to certain kinds of letters. In some ways, automation of communications has increased the quality of information included in letters. When each response does not have to be original, staff members and the congressmen alike are more likely to take some time to draft a well-developed letter, rather than dashing off a response to reduce the pile a bit.

The Repertoire of Appropriate Responses

Most offices face the opportunity to respond to constituents with a combination of dread and enthusiasm. On the one hand, an inappropriate response might make a perpetual enemy; on the other hand, a satisfactory response could make at least a short-term supporter. In general, the danger of making a mistake is greater than the opportunity to gain. The watchword is "care." The question is seldom "will we respond," but rather "how?" Communications styles vary from office to office, but some general response strategies carry over many offices.

In framing an appropriate response to issue mail, the congressional office generally holds the strategic advantage of knowing where the constituent stands before it must respond. The ability to respond most effectively to each particular letter, though, is tempered by the fact that a seemingly personal letter can show up in a newspaper or newsletter. As Morris Udall (D–AZ) suggests to new Members, "Don't ever write anything to a constituent that you wouldn't be willing to see on page one of the local paper" (Tacheron and Udall 1970, p. 76). Full and frank responses may be avoided to reduce negative response from the constituency, or because of the very real fact that bills are seldom enacted into law exactly as introduced. Too early a commitment to proposed legislation can put the Member in the embarrassing position of seeming inconsistent when later opposing a heavily amended bill with the same title. Given these real fears and shortcomings, Members use a number of common strategies.

Avoiding the Issue

Particularly early in the legislative development of an issue, Members will profusely thank the constituent for "giving me the advantage of your wise counsel" or "providing me with such irrefutable facts on which to make my judgment" without ever making a personal commitment on the issue. While such a tactic is often used when the congressman's position opposes that of the constituent, the letter usually ends with the commitment, "I will give your position my thoughtful consideration."

Reading congressional responses often gives few clues as to what the writer communicated in the first place. Many offices use the initial constituent letter as an excuse to communicate how qualified the Member is for the job, the degree to which he identifies with his constituents, his empathy for their problems, and a catalogue of his recent achievements, without ever facing up to the issue raised.

Going a bit further than the "half duck step" (Feldstein 1979, pp. 44–46), some offices use "full duck" strategies. They might try to avoid the issue by "passing the buck," claiming that they will not take a stand since the issue does not fall under their area of responsibility or that it has been bottled up in committee or in the other chamber. As with casework mail, offices will generally send issue mail from another constituency back to that Member using a "buck slip." A more subtle way of completely avoiding the issue involves inundating the writer with speeches, press releases, committee reports, and other handouts which may have only tangential relationship to the initial issue on which the constituent wrote.

Careful Ambiguity

Most members of Congress believe that you can not be criticized effectively for a stand you did not take. Members try not to take a stand on controversial issues unless and until they have to, and when taking a stand they try to "couch it in language which will lead people on all sides of the issue to respect your views or be confused as to where you actually stand" (McCloskey 1972, p. 102). Assuring constituents that their views "will be taken into account" or that the member is "currently leaning toward a solution such as the one suggested" may mean one thing to the constituent as a commitment and another to the Member. Some of the most ambiguous congressional communications emanated from congressional offices during the Watergate debate. While firmly asserting that "no man is above the law" and that "this mess must be cleaned up," many Members "reserved judgment until all the facts were in" and refused to even hint at which direction they were leaning. This was particularly effective in the Senate, where Members could effectively hide behind their status as a jury in the impeachment proceedings.

Searching for Areas of Agreement

Congressional offices begin with the general assumption that constituents seek policy compliance from members of Congress and not a stimulating dialog on the pros and cons of an issue. Thus, few Members want to communicate total disagreement. Agreeing with a constituent on the "ultimate importance of this issue" or agreeing that "action must be taken immediately" may not mean agreement on the definition of the problem or the desired remedial action, but with enough flowery adjectives it can pass for total agreement. Staff members will comb through letters for areas of agreement with the Member's position and focus on those segments to the exclusion of others.

At times this process is quite subtle. During the debate over Viet Nam, many Members realized that many of the same people concerned with our Viet Nam policy also held strong environmental concerns. Some offices began consciously to respond to anti–Viet Nam mail on recycled paper to send the signal that while we may not agree totally on Viet Nam, we are just as concerned about the environment as you are.

If the congressman has already clearly taken a public position on an issue, agreement may not be possible. In those cases the congressional office hopes to get the constituent to "agree to disagree" and go on from there. The approach often takes the form of saying, "While reasonable people can disagree on this issue, you should realize that on most other issues we are all in complete agreement." The message is clearly one of, "Don't totally break the established constituent–congressman relationship over one issue where no absolute right or wrong can be established."

Consistency

As issues pass through the legislative process, the possibility of avoiding stands diminished. While Congress protects its Members through committee sessions closed to the public (although to a lesser degree than in the past) and unrecorded votes, most issues of public concern end up with some public form of expressing support or opposition. Congressmen anticipate how they will explain their positions and votes to constituents.

Members are, of course, called upon to vote much more often than they are called upon to explain. That is, they are never called upon to explain all their votes. Their uncertainty about which votes they will have to explain, however, leads them to prepare explanations for more votes than they need to. (Fenno 1977, p. 910)

An important part of explaining one's stand is consistency. As Senator Robinson (D–KY) used to tell freshmen Members, "Gentlemen, it is better to be fur somethin' than to be agin it, but if you've got to be agin it, be everlastingly agin it" (Tacheron and Udall 1970, p. 77). While Emerson ("Essay on Self-reliance") argued that "consistency is the hobgoblin of little minds," constituents seem to forgive a congressman's being consistently "wrong" on an issue of importance to them more readily than the unnerving vacillation of a public official.

Careful Duplicity

There is a tendency to believe that anyone who would avoid a full and frank response to a constituent letter would also bow to the temptation to totally mislead different sets of constituents by saying one thing to one group and something else to another. While it is true that offices generally prepare two form letters on controversial issues, one for the pros and one for the cons, it is seldom true that such communications are directly contradictory. For example, former Senator Stephen Young (D–OH) used to reply to anti-abortion letters by saying, "I appreciate hearing from you and learning of your opposition to abortion," while the proabortion letters received the message, "I appreciate receiving your views on this matter. . . .I agree with you that a woman should have a right to decide whether or not she wants an abortion." (Feldstein 1979, p. 43)

Richard Fenno followed congressmen into their constituencies to gauge the nature of face-to-face communications with constituents and found that far from being "explanatory chameleons," Members did explain their positions in similar ways to opposing audiences, although they certainly did not go out of their way to find disagreement (Fenno 1978, pp. 157–59).

Cautious Frankness

When disagreement is clear, some Members find it advantageous to face the matter head on. They believe that a polite and well-reasoned response may catch an antagonist off guard and breed respect rather than reproach (*Congressional Quarterly* 1976, p. 534). A constituent may be so complimented that the Member took his views seriously enough to disagree that the disagreement itself is apt to be forgiven (Udall and Tacheron 1970, p. 77).

Before we herald ambiguous frankness as an unmixed blessing, two caveats deserve mentioning. First, Members of Congress who rush to make judgements early in the legislative process may find themselves without the advantage of the constituent counsel and committed to undesirable legislation; while the Members whose initial responses seem ambiguous or filled with duplicity have bought some time for contemplation and may be more responsive than the Members who firmly outline where they stand on everything. Secondly, taking a position on an issue is not necessarily the same as doing something about it, as Richard Fenno argues:

> Position taking is just as misleading to constituents and as manipulative of their desires as image selling. . . . Appearing to do something about policy without a serious intention of, or a demonstrable capacity for doing so is no less a corruption of the representative relationship . . . than is the feigning a personal relationship without a serious intention of establishing one. (Fenno 1977, p. 916)

THE IMPORTANCE OF MAIL HANDLING ROUTINES

The way in which issue mail is handled by congressional offices reveals a great deal about how those offices view the mail. The very terminology that mail is to be "handled" (rather than "analyzed," "scrutinized," etc.) implies getting rid of the stacks with the least amount of effort and the maximum political gain. The terminology indicates that many participants in the process have lost sight of the fact that the goal of issue mail is to set up a dialog between the congressional office and the constituent in the hopes of enhancing representation and responsiveness. In many offices form tends to override substance.

After describing to one of my colleagues the sophisticated manner in which responses are drafted to appease the constituent and imply personalization, I was brought back down to earth by his reaction. "I don't write my congressman to get a response, I write him to affect the course of policy decisions. Whether I receive a nicely drafted letter is immaterial. I want a representative, not a pen pal."

It is not just constituents who have qualms about how congressional offices deal with mail. Former Senator William Fulbright expressed his dissatisfaction thus:

We seem to have lost the most basic tool of communication, which is clarity of word and thought, the articulation of ideas, the analysis of problems and the exposition of programs through speech and writing. Our elected representatives and the "communications" experts they employ, study and analyze public attitudes by sophisticated new techniques, but their purpose has little to do with leadership, still less with education. Their purpose, it seems, is to discover what people want and fear and dislike, and then to identify themselves with those sentiments. (Fulbright 1979, p. 722)

In the long run, the unwillingness of many Members to grapple openly with issues and their attempts to avoid responsibility for their actions does more than mislead individual constituents. Out of fear of truly educating constituents and perhaps losing some support, Members are very selective about the information they provide and often highly critical of Congress as an institution. Thus members of Congress may actually "help depress citizen understanding of and respect for the United States Congress" (Fenno 1978, p. 169). To go a step further, current communications patterns may confuse issues, paper over important conflicts, and ultimately lead to disillusionment with the entire political process. After the letters, there ultimately comes action (or perhaps nonaction). For the constituent soothed by a letter from a congressman, undesired action on the part of either the congressman or the entire Congress may well build disillusionment.

THE POLICY CONSEQUENCES OF ISSUE COMMUNICATIONS: COUNTING AND WEIGHING THE MAIL

The concrete evidence concerning the policy impact of mail on the legislative process is spotty and inconsistent. Numerous individual Members describe cases where the mail made a difference:

[Morris Udall] On several occasions I can testify that a single, thoughtful, factually persuasive letter did change my mind or cause me to initiate a review of a previous judgment. Nearly every day my faith is renewed by one or more informative and helpful letters giving me a better understanding of the thinking of my constituents. (Udall 1967, p. 1)

Other observers argue that "isolated letters on specific matters will rarely reach the legislator's eye" (Ornstein 1972, p. 40).

On the other extreme, massive mail campaigns, such as the previously mentioned outpouring of millions of letters in opposition to withholding of interest and dividend income, were credited with turning the tide on that issue. Yet it is often argued that if Members get the hint of an organized campaign of form letters and identical postcards, they will "usually discount the responses" . (Ornstein 1972, p. 40)

In the middle ground (those issues which generate a number of letters but no overwhelming outpouring), Members keep track of the direction and intensity (by volume) of responses but are quick to point out (particularly when the letters fail to agree with the Member's positions) all the weaknesses of responding to a small number of letters probably from a unique set of constituents.

There are clearly few hard and fast rules about the impact of mail. Traditional empirical methods of correlating a potential cause (in this case mail) with congressional behavior fail for lack of data and/or the multitude of competing explanatory factors. No observer truly believes that issue mail controls legislative output, nor does anyone believe that congressional decision making goes on, isolated from the impact of constituent letters.

Some Preconditions for Policy Impact

Aware Citizens

Many of our images of U.S. citizens are either outdated or were never valid. In the early days of the Republic, the legal right to participate was limited and representatives were elected by participatory town or country meetings, "thus by political bodies with an identity and some experience in collective action. . . . Consequently, dialog between representatives and their constituencies was frequent and vigorous; representatives were often instructed and sometimes recalled" (Pitkin and Shumer 1982). In the modern age of full participation and political individualism, such an image does not ring true. As one member of Congress complained, "I don't think people could specify anything in my voting record. . . .I once printed it and offered to send it to anyone who wanted it. No one did. It was too complicated to understand."

It has become the conventional wisdom that constituents have limited policy interest and information. As one study reported:

While only about 9% of the respondents in districts with an incumbent running correctly perceived the incumbent's position in all three issue areas, another 15% were correct in two issue areas, and 23% were correct in only one area. Thus 47% were right in at least one issue area, but the majority of constituents were either incorrect in all their assessments or failed to even guess at their congressmen's positions. (Hurley and Hill 1980, p. 442)

While such figures might be staggering to those who view constituents as capable of evaluating the total policy performance of a congressman, such figures miss the mark and do not prove that constituents are policy ignorant. It is not the omniscient constituent armed with information on every position and vote who keeps a congressman on guard; it is rather the individual or group deeply concerned and having information on one narrow policy area that might have an impact (Fenno 1978, p. 142).

The attempts by outside observers to specify which issues constituents "should" be interested in often miss the mark. For a wide variety of reasons, individuals specialize in issue areas which come to their attention, and their choices may not correlate with the seemingly big issues of the day. For example, Senator Moynihan's (D-NY) 1977 mailbags included more letters about the need to save the Alaskan timber wolf than about nuclear arms (Moynihan 1981, p. 151).

Rather than impugning the level and nature of citizen interests, it seems more productive to promote methods of increasing awareness, realizing that constituent letters may highlight some of the more obscure issues which might otherwise have "fallen through the cracks."

Targeting Appropriate Decision Makers

As is typical of all large organizations, Congress has used extensive division of labor to manage its considerable work load. Most Members do not seek out problems or decisions, but rather wait until they come into the purview of their committee assignments or are forced on them by impending floor decisions. A congressman receiving a letter from a constituent early in the policy process on an issue far afield from his committee assignment is likely to simply thank the writer for his views;and file the letter away. The letter's views will be resurrected only if and when the issue comes to the floor and the Member is required to take a stand.

Effective letter writers realize this division of labor and direct their communications to those Members currently dealing with an issue. Most issue mail, particularly that generated by interest groups, goes to Members of the appropriate committees. Within the committees, Members vary in their responsiveness to mail, and communications strategies take this into account. Making the reasonable assumption that Members with weaker electoral bases use the mail to gauge public opinion more than their secure colleagues, many organizations focus their efforts on the "marginal" Members (generally defined as those receiving less than 55 percent of the vote). During the impeachment hearings in 1974, for example, the proimpeachment groups focused their efforts on those members of the Judiciary Committee who received less than 52 percent of the vote in 1972 (*Congressional Quarterly* 1974, pp. 1368–73). Since congressmen depend more on their individual constituencies than on citizens in general for support, the most potent mail technique is to inundate marginal congressmen with mail from their districts.

Timing

The legislative process follows a fixed sequence of events which can be speeded up or retarded by the participants. As a piece of legislation wends its way through subcommittees and full committees and finally to the floor of each chamber, decisions have to be made by different groups of legislators. Once a legislator makes a public commitment, it is difficult to make a change, since colleagues and constituents would view it as inconsistency—one of the deadly sins of politics. Thus, timing often determines the effectiveness of the influence of issue mail. Most constituents fail to monitor the pace of the legislative process. They find out about issues from the mass media, which tend to cover stories at the point when decisions are already made. By reacting to the news, constituent mail often comes in too late to change behavior.

One of the dramatic advantages of organized interest groups lies in their ability to carefully monitor the stages in the legislative process and stimulate mail to the appropriate committee or subcommittee Members at a point in time where commitments are not set in cement. In the absence of countervailing communications from a more random sample of constituents, the mail precipitated by an interest group serves as a surrogate measure of public opinion.

The Nature of Demands

A considerable amount of issue mail implores a congressman to solve some problem but gives little direction as to the desired action. Sacks of mail complaining about inflation and asking the congressman to ''do something about this problem'' may alert him to public concern but help little in making a decision. Congressmen live in an environment which constantly forces them to make specific choices among alternatives, few of which are clearcut as to their goals or likely consequences. The most effective issue mail supports or opposes a specific piece of legislation and outlines how its passage or blocking would affect specific kinds of individuals. The constituent who refers to legislation by number and communicates his or her knowledge about the substance has more chance to have an impact than the writer expressing vague goals and hopes.

Defining One's Constituency

> American congressmen, being career politicians, may be predisposed to
> be responsive to policy preferences of their constituencies because even
> if they have safe electoral districts, they continue to need the support
> of their primary constituencies for renomination. (Loewenberg and Pat-
> terson 1979, p..186)

Before we attempt to analyze the impact of constituency mail on a
congressman, it is important to realize that definitions of a Member's
constituency vary (see Fenno 1978, p. 27). The most obvious definition
of one's constituency is the legal or geographic boundaries established
by state legislatures from which each congressman is elected. While easy
to define, this view of constituency seldom encompasses those citizens
a congressman feels responsible to represent. In terms of affecting behavior, a congressman's constituency is more perceptual than legal.
While some Members define their constituency as broader than the legal boundaries—such as former representative Shirley Chisholm (D–NY),
who saw her job as looking out for "the underprivileged, particularly
women and blacks"—most congressmen narrow their focus of responsiveness. Within the legal constituency is an "electoral constituency"
made up of those who bother to vote, a "reelection constituency" com-
prising an individual Member's traditional supporters, and a "personal
constituency" including campaign workers and close advisors. Members
with weak electoral bases tend to define their constituencies in broader
terms and hope to expand their base of support, while secure Members
can focus their concern on a narrower segment of the legal constituency.
A citizen's potential impact as a letter writer hinges on the breadth of
a Member's definition of constituency and whether or not the individual
constituent falls within that definition. Congressional offices go to great
lengths to determine "who" is writing, and this determination often carries more import than the content of the letter.

Judging Mail Quality Versus Quantity

Recognizing the Biases in the Mail

Few congressional offices are naive enough to believe that all mail
is equal and must be evaluated at face value. Conclusions from the mail
are often discounted when they fail to match existing preconceptions or
exhibit little commitment, while other conclusions are enhanced when
staff or Member judgment implies commitment and representativeness.
In the words of one staff member:

I've lived and worked in the district all my life, and I know the politics. . . . So, when mail comes in on an issue, or when people call, I can
tell pretty much what it means—how strong opinion is, and who is involved. That's why I make sure that every letter crosses my desk, and
that I'm aware of every contact a constituent makes with our office.
When an issue comes up that touches the district, I let———know what
a pro or con vote will mean in these terms. (Ornstein 1972, p. 82)

In most offices, the initial reading of the mail involves a mail count
of the pros and cons on each issue. While such a quick overview may
give a member some feel for the issues of interest to constituents, it often masks as much as it reveals. As one Member commented, "If they
wanted me to weigh the mail, they should have elected a butcher"
(Davis 1961, p. 11).

Congressmen are interested not only in where their constituents
stand on an issue, but also (and more importantly) in the intensity of the
constituents' feelings. Members work on the reasonable assumption that
intense desires deserve more responsiveness and will affect electoral support more directly. Intensity of opinion is hard to measure directly, so
Members evaluate it indirectly according to the amount of effort required
to communicate. Spontaneous letters from constituents take the most effort and are treated with the most respect. Constituent phone calls and
telegrams are viewed with a bit less respect. Orchestrated mail, especially
low-effort postcards where the constituent has only to sign a postage-
paid, preprinted message, is viewed with about as much respect as the
effort it took the constituent to "write" (*Congressional Staff Journal* 1981).

Congressional offices evaluate the trade-offs in their responsiveness
to various forms of communications. If the number of writers sending
personal letters supporting an issue is equal to those postcard communicators who oppose it, the letter writers will have more impact. When
the numbers vary dramatically, a very high volume of postcards could
attract more attention than a very few personal letters.

Substantive Biases

It is a well-known fact that constituents who communicate with congressional offices are far from a random sample of the population. In the
first place, members can get a false sense of security unless they realize
that they will hear most from constituents who agree with them (Hinckley 1978, pp. 47–48). With the choice of three members of Congress with
whom to communicate (one representative and two senators), the typical constituent will try to get the uncommitted Member to take a stand
or reinforce the Member leaning his way before tackling the more difficult and less probable goal of changing a Member's mind.

Since letter writers tend to be higher on the socioeconomic scale (see

Chapter 2), it is not surprising that the mail better reflects their interests. On numerous issues in recent history, the mail has been out of sync with public opinion. In 1939, 56 percent of the public supported the repeal of the Neutrality Act, while over 80 percent of the congressional letter writers opposed it. In 1940, 70 percent of the public supported the Selective Service System, while 90 percent of the letter writers opposed it (*Congressional Quarterly* 1976, p. 15). When Medicare was debated, over two-thirds of the public supported it, while over two-thirds of the letter writers, who generally had their own health insurance program and whose efforts were encouraged by the American Medical Association, expressed opposition to the incursion of "socialized medicine." During the late 1960s, letter writers supported the war in Viet Nam to a much greater degree than the general population (Verba and Brody 1970, p. 331). Perhaps most instructive was the tremendous outpouring of mail on the withholding of taxes on interest and dividend income (see previous discussion), which was a classic case of the "haves" fighting and scraping to hold on to a perceived benefit and in the process sending a dramatic, if not fully representative, message to the Congress.

Although the issue mail entering Congress is biased, the distortion may well be a blessing in disguise for the Member. The mail represents the better informed, more interested, most active, and best organized constituents. These are the very citizens likely to determine the political fate of the Member, especially in low-interest primaries and off-year elections. In extreme cases, a lack of responsiveness to these individuals could lead to a challenge from within the activist elite, while the disappointment of the less active segments of the constituency is largely treated with impunity.

THE BOTTOM LINE: WHEN THE MAIL COUNTS

Attempting to assess the precise impact of issue mail is probably doomed to failure. From a methodological perspective it will always be difficult to determine whether congressmen follow constituent wishes out of fear of defeat, out of a sense of responsibility, or simply because they are transplanted locals expressing their own policy biases (Davidson and Oleszek 1981, pp. 386–87). There is considerable evidence that constituents are uninformed on most issues, that those who write are atypical, and that Members with least responsiveness to their districts do not lose consistently at the polls (Flerlage 1975, p. 2).

In assessing the impact of constituent mail on a Member's legislative stands, it is important to point out that reaction to a particular piece of legislation involves a continuum from active support to active opposition, with passive support and opposition as well as neutrality in between. While constituent letters may not move a Member from active support to active opposition, they may lead a Member to reduce his support activity and fade into the posture of simply voting for the legislation without trying to stir up support. Such a shift reflects constituent influence and could affect the ultimate outcome.

While it would be unwarranted to conclude that constituent mail has a consistent and determinative impact on congressional decision making, the opposite position that mail never makes a difference is also clearly unwarranted. Constituent mail is a kind of "wild card" in the legislative process. Few people can predict when and where it will appear, or whether it will have an impact; but after the fact its impact on a specific decision becomes clear. Part of the problem in analyzing mail is that we have some faulty perceptions on what mail should and can do.

The Rational Decision Making Fallacy

Most observers of Congress would like to believe that it follows a strict rational model of decision making in which goals are set, full information gathered on the means to each goal, and options chosen. The legislative process is a bit more messy. Goals are often ill-defined and conflicting. Full information, especially as it relates to constituent desires, is seldom available. Decisions on means to reach a goal are often tentative "trial balloons," where a seemingly final decision generates more information rather than putting the issue to rest.

Realistic Functions of Constituent Mail

Constituent Mail and Agenda Setting

Letters from constituents can serve as a stimulus to put an issue on the public agenda. As the late Congressman Clem Miller described it:

> Sometimes a volume of mail seems to force an issue to a conclusion without seeming to have any particular effect on the actual result. The Labor Bill is a good case in point. The agitation for a labor bill pushed the House Committee on Education and Labor to take some sort of action. Our mail was not much help in deciding exactly what should be done. (Miller 1962, p. 72)

While most legislation originates in the executive branch, interest groups, or congressional committees, there have been numerous cases where one letter stimulated a Member to introduce legislation with national implications. The fact that women are now admitted to the military academies was the result of one high school girl complaining that she was not being given an equal opportunity to the benefit of a free education. The Pension Reform Bill was sparked by one constituent whose employer went out of business when the constituent was 64, causing the constituent's pension to disappear with the company.

At times, Members use letters as bargaining tools during floor debate. It is common debate technique to report mail counts or actually brandish sheaves of letters at fellow Members to prove constituent interest.

Constituent Mail and Full Information

The great respect with which congressmen treat constituent mail reflects less on its quality and comprehensiveness than on the inadequacies of other information sources on the quality of legislation and its likely impact. If members of Congress had adequate and timely public opinion polls of their constituencies which allowed them to determine the opinions of the relevant parts, constituent mail would be superfluous. Lacking such information, congressmen grasp at any available straws to mold their perceptions of constituent interests. While congressmen vary in their opinions of the need to be responsive to their constituents, none wants unknowingly to spurn constituent desires. If congressmen's judgments lead them to different conclusions, they would at least like to know the stands they will have to explain. Constituent mail, while not necessarily providing direct information on constituent desires, serves as one of the components of a congressman's perception of the constituency. ''Unlike the private citizen, the congressman does not distort his perceptions to coincide with his own attitudes, because the costs of misperceiving are so high for an elected official'' (Cnudde and McCrone 1961, p. 72).

Thus, while filtered through the judgments and evaluations of the congressmen and their staff, the mail serves as an indirect piece of information affecting legislative decisions. In those few cases where mail is overwhelming, timely, and specific, its uniqueness assures it a dramatic role.

Constituent Mail as Reaction

In many cases, congressional decisions reached on the basis of little or no constituent mail impact become caught in a maelstrom of reaction reflected in the mail. Numerous examples exist of legislative action being reversed by the mail. After the Senate voted with little citizen awareness to add a $4 million gym to the Hart Office Building, it was not long before congressional mailbags were filled with letters expressing vitriol at the decision. "The Senate, seeing the error in its ways in an election year, recanted, voting 98 to 0 to mothball the gym" (*Washington Post* 1982, p. a15). One Member expressed his experience on another bill in this way:

> I sponsored a bill to increase the size of trucks on our highways. But I got an awful lot of mail on that and it would have lost me a lot of people.... Confidentially, I tell you it was a good bill; and I'm still in favor of it. But because so many people were opposed to it, I decided not to support it. I'm not here to vote my own convictions. I'm here to represent my people. (Fenno 1978, p. 146)

The reversal of Congress's position on the plan to withhold taxes on interest and dividend income—which we have already discussed—is another example of how mail can unexpectedly appear after the fact and change the course of the legislative process.

The very fact that certain issues can catch the fancy of the public and unexpectedly generate a deluge of mail enhances the mail's potency. While hard to predict and difficult to explain, constituent letters can selectively affect the outcome of some issues. In such a situation, constituents desiring to affect public policy would be well advised to follow the late Congressman Clem Miller's suggestion to his constituents:

> My counsel to everyone who asked was to write. One letter might spark an entirely new line of thought or endeavor. I can think of several issues last session upon which particular letters gave me a fresh or definitive focus. (Miller 1962, p. 71)

CHAPTER 6

EXPANDING OUTREACH:
Unsolicited Communications

> Member-initiated communications provide perhaps the best available as-
> surance that Members will reach all of their constituents with the im-
> ages of themselves that they wish to portray.... Such communications
> are probably the only way in which Members reach a majority of their
> constituents in the inter-election period. (Yiannakis 1979, p. 2)

> Member's offices resemble the mail distribution division of a large busi-
> ness. Every day stacks of printed matter are released for wide distribu-
> tion. Materials include press releases, newsletters, individual and mass
> mailings, and programs or tapes for electronic media. (Davidson and
> Oleszek 1981, p. 139)

Congressmen and their staffs would like to have you think that extreme emphasis on constituent communications and the increase in outgoing mail volume stems solely from constituent demands. In reality mail
volume is also related to increased efficiency and regular congressional
encouragement. Efficient mail handling leads to quicker responses, which
in turn encourage repeated correspondence. Many offices develop almost
a "pen pal" relationship with a fair number of constituents. The image
of the office manager bemoaning the amount of mail must be balanced
against the direct solicitation of future communications in newsletters and
the standard closing line of much congressional correspondence, "Feel
free to contact me again on this or any other matter." The amount and
nature of what arrives in the congressional mailbags is in large part a
function of what goes out. Outgoing mail begets increased incoming
mail, which in turn provides more opportunities for the congressional
office to increase its outgoing mail once again. This is not an entirely new
phenomenon, as Charles Clapp reported over two decades ago:

Although there are frequent complaints that the volume of mail is too heavy, and that much of it is unnecessary...everyone on Capitol Hill will tell you it is important. Once a congressman becomes accustomed to a heavy mail, he tends to worry if it drops off.... Many congressional mass mailings are designed to get recipients to write to the congressman, and a large mailing list is a source of much pride. (Clapp 1963, p. 75)

THE PURPOSE OF CONGRESSIONAL OUTREACH

The major purpose of congressional outreach mail is to break through the barriers of ignorance and apathy in order to bring its message to those people not normally attuned. Congressmen are quick to conclude, "We don't really get through to our people through the media" (congressman, quoted in Tacheron and Udall 1970, p. 115). As one long-time Capitol Hill correspondent put it, "People who want to participate in the political process are already involved, but those who don't tune in now, still won't tune in in the future.... Congressional offices will still need gimmicks." (Don Philips, quoted in Haskell 1982, p. 50). Once congressmen get through to the less involved, the message is quite simple. They wish to assert their concern for the constituents' problems and opinions and to affirm that they and their staffs are ready and willing to serve. The difficulty is getting past the barriers of inattention and lack of concern.

OUTREACH METHODS

Congressional offices spare little effort and creativity in establishing lines of communication with their constituents. The ability to establish personal contact with constituents through face-to-face meetings is most potent, but also very costly in terms of the congressman's scarcest resource, time. Extensive research on congressmen's trips back to their districts indicates that there has been a linear increase in the amount of time the average member spends in the district, and that individual variation is closely related to the member's electoral needs. District trips clearly increase during election periods, particularly for members in the deepest political trouble (Fenno 1978, p. 209; Parker 1980, passim).

In order to more wisely shepherd their limited time, congressmen have increasingly relied on surrogate communicators in the form of district offices. In the not-so-distant past, the Washington D.C. office was the hub of all activity and an office in the district a rarity; today, however, congressmen average two offices per district (Cranor and Westphal 1978, p. 6). Many offices take the district office concept one step further by using motor homes to create a mobile office which can bring the office to the people.

While these approaches to increasing a dialog (or at least a monolog) with the people, are important, our focus is on the more impersonal, albeit more efficient, methods by which Members can attempt to create communications links with much larger percentages of their constituencies through the mails. What is lost in intensity is expected to be gained in spread of coverage. The primary vehicles for such communications are newsletters, polls, and targeted mailing lists.

Newsletters

The congressional newsletter printed and mailed at government expense is the most common method by which members of Congress attempt to bring their messages to the broadest number of constituents. While always popular in the modern Congress, it has become almost a universally used technique. (see Figure 6.1). Currently the variation is not over whether an office sends out newsletters, but rather over the frequency and content of the newsletters. The average Member sends out almost one newsletter every other month (Bond 1983, p.11), with some Members contacting constituents once a month. House members have it much easier since they are allowed to send postal patron mailings to each address in their constituency, while senators are required to use discrete addresses. Once of the reasons the Senate has been considering going to the postal patron approach is the tremendous effort senatorial offices put into correcting their mailings lists for rejected and undeliverable mail. The volume of bad addresses is so great that many offices simply cannot keep up, and newsletters are repeatedly returned month after month (Mathias 1982a, p. S11333). As with the more personal forms of communications, the frequency of newsletters is clearly related to the electoral marginality of the Member (Cover 1980, p. 6).

To some degree the sending of newsletters is as much a matter of form as of substance. The fact that the Member has attempted to communicate overshadows to some degree the content of the communication. This does not mean that Members pay little attention to the content. They hedge their bets and optimistically assume that the newsletter will make it off the dining room table and be digested carefully by the majority of constituents. Newsletters tend to be

> upbeat accounts of the legislator's activities, complete with photos of
> the legislator greeting constituents or conferring with top decision-

FIGURE 6.1

THE GROWTH IN NEWSLETTER USAGE BY HOUSE OFFICES
(percentage of offices sending newsletters)

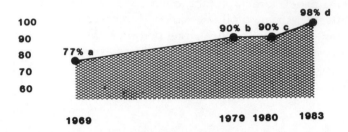

SOURCES:
[a]Saloma 1969, p. 309.
[b]Green 1979, p. 309.
[c]Cover 1980, p. 129.
[d]Bond 1983, p. 11.

makers...Recipients are urged to share their views or contact local offices for help. Perhaps once a year, the newsletter may feature an opinion poll asking for views on selected issues. Whatever the results, the underlying message is that the legislator really cares what folks back home think. (Davidson and Oleszek 1981, p. 142)

As one Member of Congress described it:

I do believe that it [newsletters] helped me more in vote-getting than any single thing I did that I kept them advised. They don't ask for weighty information. They don't ask that you agree with them.... What they do want is to know that you care enough about them to write home and that makes a big hit, that you are still aware of the fact that they sent you here. (Tacheron and Udall 1970, p. 116)

One study of newsletter content revealed that close to 40 percent of the Members used newsletters for self-promotion, while less than a quarter of the Members used newsletters for persuasion on the issues or objective education (William Love, quoted in Green 1979, p. 277).

Newsletter content seems to be related most clearly to the nature of the district:

The poorer the district, the more the representative claims credit for particularized benefits, while the richer and more homogeneous the district, the more positions the member takes, and can safely take them, on national issues. (Yiannakis 1979, p. 27)

Realizing the political benefits of newsletters, and under pressure from such groups as Common Cause, both the House and Senate have tried to limit the cases of extreme misuse of newsletters, while maintaining the Member's flexibility for keeping in touch with constituents. Both chambers limit mailings close to election day and have standards limiting the number of pictures of the Member and personal pronouns in each newsletter. Directly asking for contributions or votes is also prohibited (Himowitz 1982). While these are important signals, the process is largely one of self-policing.

A recent court case involving Senator Proxmire's charges against a scientist with a government grant weakened Members' newsletter rights. The court ruled that while Senator Proxmire was protected against libel in announcing his "Golden Fleece" awards on the floor, informing functions such as newsletters, while legitimate activities, are political in nature rather than legislative and therefore not protected. Proxmire was found guilty of libel for his newsletter and fined (Kennedy 1980, p. 730).

While closer scrutiny of the frank and of the content of newsletters may well change the practices of a few members, differentiating the political and the informing functions of newsletters is impossible. Newsletters give the incumbent a dramatic advantage in keeping his name in front of the public and informing it on the issues and accomplishments he desires. Even in the early campaign period, the newsletter is a dramatic weapon. One Member proclaimed: "It's dramatically easier to run as an incumbent. My opponent made a vicious attack on me in his announcement statement, and I answered it the following day by mailing 220,000 newsletters." (Bibby 1983, p. 46).

Constituent Polls

The Purpose of Polls

The popularity of soliciting constituent opinion through newsletter polls has increased dramatically in recent years. The practice, used by less than 12 percent of congressional offices in the 1950s, now finds application by over 75 percent of the offices (Erickson 1980, p. 251). While Members argue that polls provide them with new information (Wilcox 1966, pp. 528–32) and contribute to the government responsibility to "stimulate public concentration on governmental affairs" (Congressman Ed Derwinski, quoted in Wilcox 1966, p. 532), these purposes take a back seat to the more potent political motivations. Congressional polling is a clear case of form superceding substance. The act of soliciting constituent opinions is more important "for letting constituents know the Congressman cares about district attitudes" (Fox and Hammond 1977, p. 114) than for its utility in policy guidance (see Table 6.1). "Congressmen believe questionnaires win friends in their districts" (*Congressional Quarterly* 1976, p. 538). Poll results would have to be a rather one-sided surprise before a Member would consider them a factor in policy decisions.

Methodological Shortcomings of Polls

Even if a congressman desired to use a poll for policy guidance, the typical deadly methodological flaws would result in more misguidance than guidance. Few congressional staff members have the skills or resources to produce a valid poll even if they want to. In the first place, congressional questionnaires break many of the basic polling rules of random sampling. Using the typical method of including the questionnaire in a newsletter sent to all households, it is quite uncommon to have more than ten percent returned. While 15,000 responses may seem like a large amount of information with which to make a judgment, those people who selected themselves into the sample by taking the effort to respond are likely to be some of the most interested and extreme members of the constituency. A recent study comparing congressional poll respondents with the results of a random sampling indicated that congressional polls represent the Member's most ardent supporters but not the constituency as a whole, nor even those people who voted for the Member (Stolarek et al. 1981).

If the samples reveal flaws, the questions are often worse. They often lead the respondent to a particular answer through biased wording and prestige endorsements. Most people want to be with the majority and react favorably or negatively to particular words. The following clearly biased questions were used by members of Congress with expected results:

> By a vote of 290 to 130 the House passed, and the Senate is now debating the civil rights bill proposed by President Kennedy and strongly supported by President Johnson. From what you know of it, do you generally favor or oppose the bill? (Udall 1964, p. 22447)

> The Constitution established the Congress as the legislative branch of government, the co-equal and independent of the executive and judicial branches. A drive has recently been announced to destroy the independence of the Congress by purging Congressmen who refuse to be rubber stamps for the executive arm of government. Would you want your representative in Congress to surrender to the purge threat and

TABLE 6.1
COMPARATIVE UTILITY OF VARIOUS INFORMATION
SOURCES FOR POLICY DECISION MAKING
(percentage classifying source as "very helpful")

	Member Ratings[a]	Staff Ratings[b]
Staff	49	41
Executive agencies	16	7
Colleagues*	9	38
Constituent mail	n.a.	24
Constituent polls	1	9

*"Dear Colleague" letters for staff.
n.a. not available.
SOURCES:
[a]U.S. Congress, House. Commission on Administrative Review 1977, p. 671.
[b]Ibid., p. 1090.

become a rubber-stamped Congressman? YES__NO__ (From a poll prepared by Congressman John Dowdy [D–TX], quoted in Wilcox 1966, p. 527)

Do you believe merging our Army, Navy, and Air Force into a single Military Service would increase efficiency, reduce waste and duplication of effort and material, and remove inter-service rivalry? YES 77%, NO 18%, UNDECIDED 5% (From a poll by Congressman Walter Norblad [R–OR], quoted in Wilcox 1966, p. 532)

The power of a prestige endorsement for a particular stance was tested by two members from similar districts in California. One Member preceded the basic question concerning a joint U.S.-Russian space effort with a lengthy quote from John Kennedy and received a rather surprising 50 percent favorable response. The other Member did not use the Kennedy quote and received only a 34 percent favorable response (Wilcox 1966, p. 533).

While the congressional questionnaire is here to stay, it should be recognized more as a vehicle for establishing a feeling of connection for the constituent than as a true measure of constituent opinion.

Targeted Mailings

Most methods available to members of Congress for communicating with constituents are rather "blunt" instruments requiring the Member to disseminate a rather general message to a broad audience in a "shotgun" manner, in the hope that some of the information will fall on receptive targets. Broad base questionnaires, press releases, or polls may not touch on the issues of relevance to the recipient and may therefore be ignored or rejected. In the hopes of getting through the natural screens by which individuals shield themselves from unwanted communications, congressional offices increasingly turn to targeted mailing approaches which use a "rifle" approach to bring the appropriate message to the right people.

Creating a Mailing List

At the heart of an effective targeted mailing campaign is the determination of which people will be responsive to which messages. On the simplest level, congressional offices keep track of who has written them on which issues and keep those people informed on those issues as they develop. While once a nightmare of cross-referencing hard copies of letters, this process has been greatly facilitated by computerization. Today the constituent who is writing a Member will be entered into a mailing file according to the current issue position or casework request, previous communications, and any other scraps of information available from the letter (occupation, group memberships, portion of the district, etc.). Incoming mail provides a useful resource. As former Congressman David Stockman (R–MI) describes it:

> The spinoff is what most people want. Most Members don't want a lot of information about issues. They've already made up their minds, and they don't think they need it. What they want is that computer building up the lists of people they can communicate with, learning what the special interests of those people are so they can inundate them with follow-up mail. It is a very political business. What you do is segment the electorate into what they are interested in and then bombard them with mailings written in a way to elicit a favorable response. (quoted in Perry 1978, p. 1)

Massive mailings by interest groups provide the Member with a golden opportunity not only to expand his or her mailing list, but also to circumvent some of the mailing regulations. "Members of Congress who are nearing an election are strictly limited in the mailings they can send constituents at government expense, but there is no limit on answering the mail they receive" (Keller 1982).

In the Senate, mailing list creation and upkeep is currently handled by a centralized correspondence management system which allows Members to store names on the basis of up to 2,400 customized professional codes, including everything from religion and ethnic group to issue positions and previous contacts with the office. The shift to microcomputers will give Senate offices more control over their lists and the ability to tailor communications strategies more to their perceived needs. While list categories and uses are supposed to be applied for "official purposes" in informing constituents, and purely political categories such as party identification and past contributions are not supposed to be saved at public expense, little monitoring takes place. On the House side, mailing list creation is monitored even less, since each Member can contract with outside vendors or create an in-house mailing operation. Today, close to 90 percent of congressional offices utilize targeted mailing lists (Haskell 1982, p. 49), with House offices often having mailing lists with over 30,000 names (*Congressional Quarterly* 1979, p. 146) and Senate lists often topping 100,000. Lists of such magnitude obviously cannot be created from incoming communications alone. Increasingly, Members are reaching out to buy or borrow names for their lists.

Chamber rules allow the use of public funds to purchase names from outside sources, based on the arugment that Members have a legitimate function to communicate with constituents and should use all possible approaches to expand the efficiency and spread of their communications (Lightman 1979). Sources of lists run from the rather mundane acquisition of voter registration of driver's license lists to more creative targeting possible through acquiring lists of professional licensees (hunters, barbers, dentists, etc.), federal grant recipients, specialized magazine subscribers, or organization members. Many of these lists are free for the asking. Some groups will exchange lists with you. For a fee, numerous list brokers and managers will create a specialized list and "merge and purge" a set of lists either to remove duplicates, or determine the names of people sharing characteristics of different lists (Haydon 1980, pp. 43–44). The potential for tailoring lists to one's needs is limited only by resources and creativity. When former Senator Robert Griffith (R–MI) wanted to communicate with antibussing constituents in areas where he had weak electoral support, he selected all Democratic counties, dropped the black census tracts, and used the motor vehicle registration data to select individuals with new model cars, under the assumption that he would then be communicating with the upper-income (and therefore more antibussing) segements of those census tracts (Arieff 1979, p. 447). As John Eddinger, press secretary to Senator Mathias (R–MD) states it, "Congressional-constituent communications have moved swiftly and massively into direct mail programs which rival catalog-merchandising activities (Haskell 1982, p. 49).

Using the Lists

Once offices have the lists, the next challenge lies in using them creatively to spread the Member's name, accomplishments, and ideas. The goal is to get beyond the normal pool of communicators and reach those individuals who are outside the existing communications network. Lists of new mothers gleaned from newspaper birth announcements are one of the key entrees to establishing communications:

> One steady contributor to the stream of outgoing franked mail is the 72-page government pamphlet, *Infant Care*. Currently in its sixth edition, this pamphlet is among the most popular government documents available. More than 59 million copies have been printed since the pamphlet was first published in 1914. Of the three million families in the United States who had newly born children last year, roughly one-third received a free copy of the pamphlet in a plain brown wrapper with a congressional frank. (Cover and Brumberg 1982, p. 349)

High school graduates often receive a seemingly personalized congratulatory letter from the congressman, often with a calendar or other trinket. "Home district newspapers may be so carefully clipped that no new tenderfoot Boy Scout, bathing beauty, or bake-off contest winner goes unremarked by the Congressman" (McCloskey 1972, p. 107). Not only do these communications build links of awareness and indebtedness, but the names also fatten the mailing list pool. Senator Jim Sasser (D–TN) compared old and new voter registration lists and sent out thousands of letters commending people for registering (Shapiro 1982). Using specialized geographic codes or zip codes, Members can combine mailed communications with other approaches. One Member's strategy is based on the following:

> We send out 9,000 or 10,000 letters in each area telling them when I'll be there. Each person who comes gets five minutes with the congressman. About forty people come, but several thousand know we have been around and know they could see me if they wished. Politically, that's more important than the forty. (Member of Congress, quoted in Fenno 1978, p. 239)

If the individuals on a particular list share narrow enough concerns, the Member can send them a "thought you might like to know" letter each time some action is taken in Congress on a topic in their area of concern. Increasingly, Members are creating long-term mailing strategies to assure that each constituent group will receive regular mailings on topics of interest. One Member, for example, divided his constituency into 100 areas of concern and tried to communicate with each group at least every three months. When he realized that he was past his deadline for the citrus growers and that nothing of importance had happened since the last communication, he undauntedly had a short speech about the importance of the citrus industry inserted into the *Congressional Record* and sent out government-subsidized reprints of this speech. His office prides itself in sending out an average of 700 targeted letters every day, seven days a week.

Members of Congress can tap other government resources to augment their outreach. Congressman Stan Parris (R–VA) "borrowed" an employee of the Social Security Administration to develop a Social Security information booklet and help identify the 40,000 senior citizens in his district. Each was sent a copy emblazoned with the message, "Compliments of Your Congressman, Stan Parris" (Saperstein 1982, p. a1).

Many Members bring their correspondence records along with them when they go back to the district. Before each meeting they review who has written and can then comment, "Oh, yes, you wrote me a few months ago about....," or "I just got a letter from one of your neighbors...asking me about..." (Perry 1978, p. 33; *Congressional Quarterly* 1976, p. 534).

Constituents identified through incoming mail or careful targeting as having interest in specific legislation may get a letter announcing subcommittee action, another when the legislation goes to the full committee, a third announcing the Member's intention to agree with their wishes on the floor, and a reprint of his statement explaining his vote. Once a Member has some hint as to a constituent's interests, and assumedly his basis for voting, he takes the golden opportunity to personalize his contacts under the well-grounded assumption that such an approach will be most likely to create a positive image (Bond 1983, p. 17).

THE IMPLICATIONS OF TARGETED MAIL

On the positive side, targeting specific audiences and communicating narrow messages provides an efficient method of opening congressional-constituency channels of communication on issues of particular interest to the constituent. On the other hand, while few members would take the considerable risk of sending contradictory messages to different groups, targeting contributes to a segmental view of policymaking and feeds the continuation of organized and unorganized single-issue groups. While it is natural for individuals to specialize their concerns in a complex society, one of the goals of politics is to bring about compromise and accommodation among conflicting goals. If a constituent only hears from a congressman on issues where they agree, he gets a false picture of the political process and may be hampered in his ability to affect outcome on issues where he and the congressman disagree.

The representative process becomes one whole closed circle in which the government feeds the cues it has carefully cultivated the public to give. Nothing could be a more serious threat to genuine democracy. (Miller 1983, p. 21)

If one worries about the insulated political environment of congressional incumbents, targeted mailings have become one of the chief resources available to them for building political support with little risk. The problem is exacerbated by the legal precedents that the individual Member retains proprietary rights to the lists and can control their use, even though they were created at public expense (Staenberg 1977, p. 22). New Members, especially after defeating or replacing an incumbent of another party, are generally faced with beginning the list-building process anew. Although the existing lists would still be useful for keeping constituents informed, their political value means that they will not be shared, and the constituent becomes the pawn in the power struggle. In a more direct political sense:

> These special mailing lists have another important advantage. Congressmen cannot send explicitly campaign-related material at public expense. What they can do is have a computer firm work up special mailing lists for official congressional material. Then when the time comes for campaign mailings, the congressman can go back to the same firm and buy the same list with campaign money, at much less expense than an opponent who would need to work up specialized lists afresh. (Perdue 1977, p. 54)

There is little question that targeted mailings work. Constituents like the personalization and reward the Member making the effort. Targeted mailings encourage more first-time communications from constituents than do traditional mass mailings. The remaining ethical question is whom do targeted mailings benefit more, the constituent being informed or the congressmen building support?

SUMMARY

While members of Congress once sat back and waited for the incoming mail and largely limited their effort to responding, the contemporary approach is to be proactive rather than reactive. The outreach efforts of most congressional offices overshadow the time and effort expended on responding to specific requests. The growth in outgoing mail can to a large degree be explained by the increase of mass mailings. Whether the Member relies on newsletters, polls, or targeted mailings, he bypasses the press with its tendency to ignore what the Member wants to communicate and highlight what he would rather avoid and can establish a personal connection with his constituents.

CHAPTER 7

EXCEPTIONS TO THE RULE:
Humor and Brilliance

By and large, a letter to a member of Congress and the official response are taken quite seriously by both constituents and congressional offices. Constituents expend the effort to write on serious problems, and congressional offices both recognize the constituents' concerns and understand the political implications of not taking their communications seriously. A perusal of either incoming or outgoing mailbags would seldom precipitate descriptions such as "exciting" or "humorous." Once in a while, though, the normal pattern is broken by a creative, bumbling, or disturbed constituent, and the congressional office is able to respond in an atypical manner.

The letters used in this chapter are all authentic, but in some cases the names have been changed or deleted to protect the individuals involved. While the letters are clearly atypical of the daily fare of incoming and outgoing mail, they serve the purpose of defining the range of mail, while placing in clearer focus the typical letter which is seriously presented, carefully argued, and taken quite seriously.

SURPRISES IN THE INCOMING MAIL BAG

Clever Humor

In a setting where real conflict over goals and serious personal concerns rule the day, creative use of humor can make a point more dramatically than a serious tome on the same subject, as the following three letters prove (Figures 7.1–7.3):

FIGURE 7.1

July 26, 1982

Dear Senator,

My freind Boreaux over in Pima County recieved a $1000 check from the Government this year for not raising hogs. So I am going into the not-raisings business next year. What I want to know is, in your opinion, what is the best kind of hogs not to raise? I would prefer not to raise Razorbacks, but, if there is no other good breed to not raise, I will just as gladly raise Bershires or Durocs.

The hardest work in this business is going to be in keeping an inventory of how many hogs I haven't raised. My freind Bordeaux is very joyful about the future of this business. He has been raising hogs for more than 20 years and the best he ever made was $400 until this year, when he got $1,000 for not raising hogs. If I can get $1,000 for not raising 50 hogs, then I will get $2,000 for not raising 100 hogs.

I plan to oeprate on a small scale at first, holding myself down to about 4,000 hogs, which means I will have $8,000. Now, another thing: These hogs I will not raise will not eat 100,000 bushels of corn. I understand that you also pay farmers for not raising 100,000 bushels of corn not to feed the hogs I am not raising? I want to get started as soon as possible as this seems to be a good time of the year for not raising hogs.

Thank you

P.S.

If you know of any other programs that will pay me not to produce I sure would appreciate it.

SOURCE: Personal Member file.

Unintended Humor

While humor may be a clever strategy, many of the "chuckles" in congressional offices come from constituent letters which are not intended to be funny. As Figures 7.4–7.10 demonstrate, misconceptions about government and poor choice of words often result in humor:

FIGURE 7.2

London, Ohio
July 26, 1967

Congressman Clarence J. Brown, Jr.
Washington, D.C.

Dear Sir:

I have a dependent relative who has very little fiscal responsibility. He means well, but he keeps buying presents for my parents and me, charging them to our account!
When he sees something that he thinks we might need, he buys it and we have to pay. These things are rarely what we'd have bought ourselves. Because he doesn't work for a living, money doesn't mean much to him. He is generous to the poor and needy, with my money--and gives to the unworthy, too.
We just received a bill for his last spending spree, and it gives me a sick, hopeless feeling. How much better things would be if we could spend our own money for the things we want!
He won't listen to me, but he will listen to you. Please, please use your influence to cut the spending of my Uncle Sam.
Truly yours,
Reimund Manneck

FIGURE 7.3

Dear Congressman:

Some ninny working for the government has informed me that under the law, oats are not a feed grain. Would you please explain that to my mule? I sure can't.

Sincerely,

SOURCE: Skubik, 1968, p. 63.

SOURCE: Congressional Quarterly 1976, p. 542.
Reprinted by permission.

FIGURE 7.5

Senator Kenneth Keating
Senate Office
Washington, D. C.

Dear Senator:

I have an important problem that I would like
to talk over with some high ranking government
officials. Please arrange as soon as possible an
appointment for me to see President Eisenhower,
the Attorney General and J. Edgar Hoover. I would
also like to see you, but I know how busy you are.

Felix I

FIGURE 7.4

Dear Congressman Akerrotty,

I received your letter and also your book.
It just aint so about me having a baby.
There was a woman down the road here
that had a baby. They are trying to
put it on my husband, John. He say
it aint so, but I dont know. Now
the news is all the way to
Washington.

SOURCE: Lowell 1960, p. 82.

FIGURE 7.6

SOURCE: Skubik 1968, p. 53.
(Response of constitu-
ent receiving a copy of
Infant and Baby Care)

Veterans Administration
Washington, D. C.

Madam:

My husband is a veteran and is receiving
partial disability whereas he is totally
disabled.
    If you could spend one night with my hus-
band you would realize that he is entitled to
the full amount.

Yours truly,
Mrs. George N

SOURCE: Lowell 1960, p. 131.

FIGURE 7.7

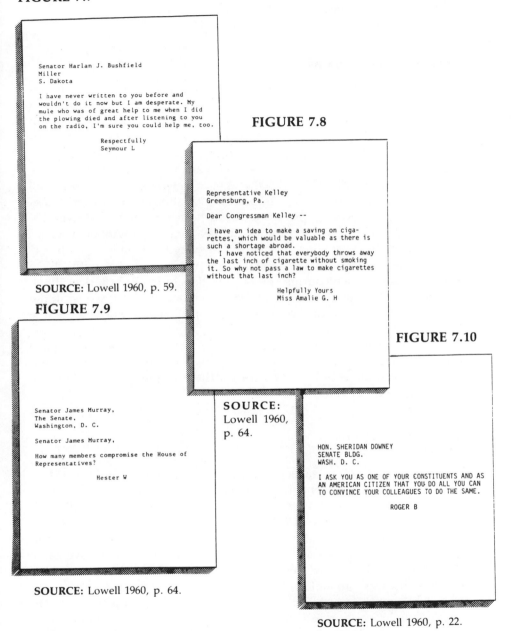

```
Senator Harlan J. Bushfield
Miller
S. Dakota

I have never written to you before and
wouldn't do it now but I am desperate. My
mule who was of great help to me when I did
the plowing died and after listening to you
on the radio, I'm sure you could help me, too.

                    Respectfully
                    Seymour L
```

FIGURE 7.8

```
Representative Kelley
Greensburg, Pa.

Dear Congressman Kelley --

I have an idea to make a saving on ciga-
rettes, which would be valuable as there is
such a shortage abroad.
    I have noticed that everybody throws away
the last inch of cigarette without smoking
it. So why not pass a law to make cigarettes
without that last inch?

                    Helpfully Yours
                    Miss Amalie G. H
```

SOURCE: Lowell 1960, p. 59.

FIGURE 7.9

```
Senator James Murray,
The Senate,
Washington, D. C.

Senator James Murray,

How many members compromise the House of
Representatives?

                    Hester W
```

SOURCE: Lowell 1960, p. 64.

FIGURE 7.10

```
HON. SHERIDAN DOWNEY
SENATE BLDG.
WASH. D. C.

I ASK YOU AS ONE OF YOUR CONSTITUENTS AND AS
AN AMERICAN CITIZEN THAT YOU DO ALL YOU CAN
TO CONVINCE YOUR COLLEAGUES TO DO THE SAME.

                    ROGER B
```

SOURCE:
Lowell 1960,
p. 64.

SOURCE: Lowell 1960, p. 22.

At times, the congressional office can return humor with humor as the interchange in Figure 7.11 indicates.

Unique Communications

In an attempt to get the attention of members of Congress, some constituent groups send symbolic material in the mail. Supporters of a group in favor of air bag legislation sent each member their own obituaries to prove their point. Over 40,000 citizens sent nickels to the 83 House Members wavering about the creation of an agency for consumer representation, arguing that it would cost each citizen only five cents to create such an agency (Green 1979, p. 308). Senator Moynihan (D–NY) reported receiving hundreds of tea bags to protest "taxation without representation," blocks of wood to protest reduced housing starts, and over 400 old keys with the message "unlock the economy" (Moynihan 1981, p. 165). One of the most concerted efforts to sway the Congress with surprises in the mail bag was the 800,000 pie plates imprinted with "Save School Lunches" sent during the budget debate in 1983 (Barker 1983). During the school prayer debate in 1984, senators opposing prayer in the schools received thousands of telegrams from "Satan," such as the one in Figure 7.12

An official in the congressional post offices stated, "After what I have seen come through the mail, I don't think I could ever be surprised again. From oranges with messages on them to pieces of lumber, we have seen and delivered them all."

"Kook" Letters

While most offices take great pains not to disparage citizens in general or their constituents in particular, virtually every office has a file of "kook" letters. No matter how ridiculous, undecipherable, or "off-the-wall" the initial letter from a constituent, it is usually responded to politely. After a while, staff members begin to realize that they are dealing with individuals having outrageous opinions or in need of psychiatric help. Many of the "kook" letters are unfathomable tirades or "stream-of-consciousness" monologs having little relation to reality. One well-known "kook" wrote hundreds of letters on everything from matchbooks to toilet paper rolls, arguing that his breakfast cereal made noise and he was convinced that it had been bugged by the CIA. Demanding a congressional investigation, he interpreted lack of enthusiasm from

FIGURE 7.11

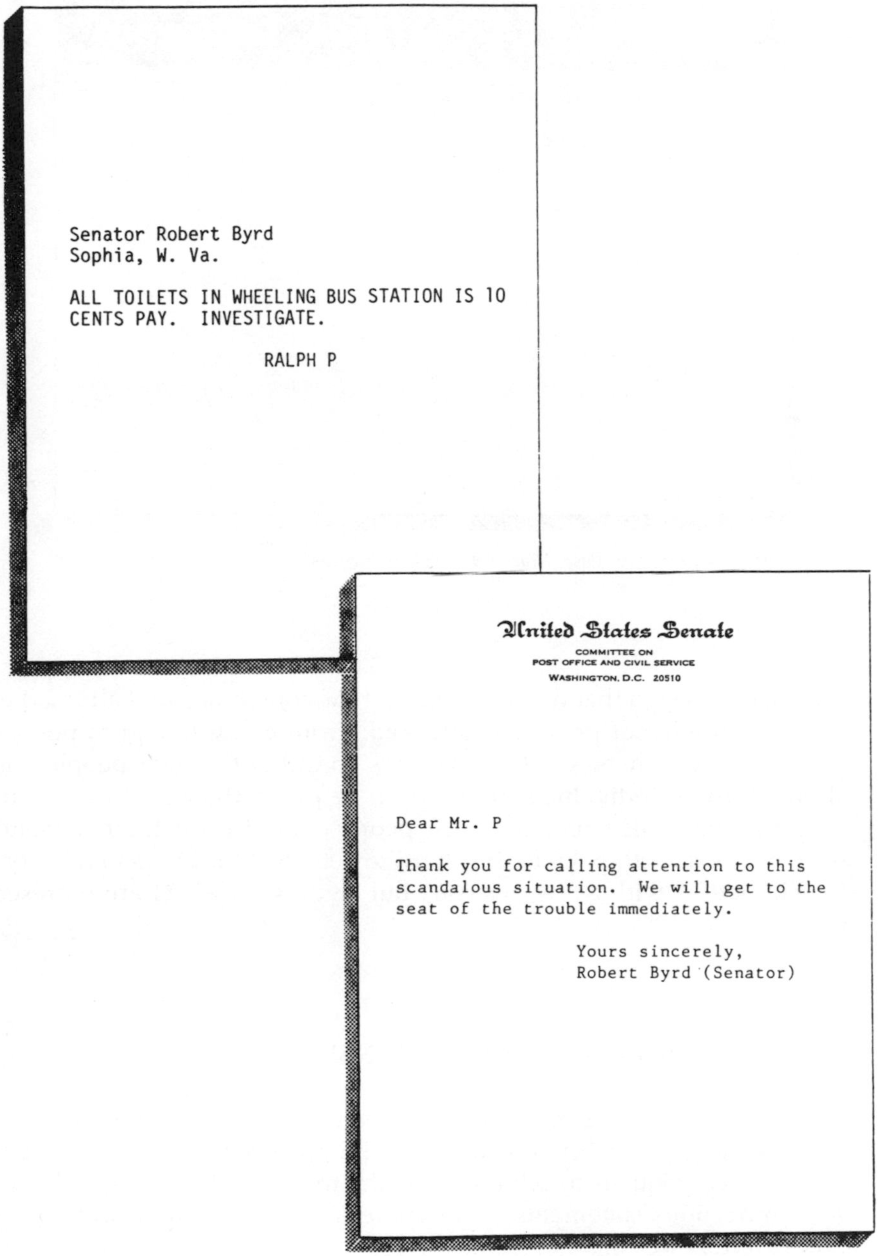

Senator Robert Byrd
Sophia, W. Va.

ALL TOILETS IN WHEELING BUS STATION IS 10
CENTS PAY. INVESTIGATE.

RALPH P

United States Senate
COMMITTEE ON
POST OFFICE AND CIVIL SERVICE
WASHINGTON, D.C. 20510

Dear Mr. P

Thank you for calling attention to this
scandalous situation. We will get to the
seat of the trouble immediately.

Yours sincerely,
Robert Byrd (Senator)

SOURCE: Lowell 1960.

FIGURE 7.12

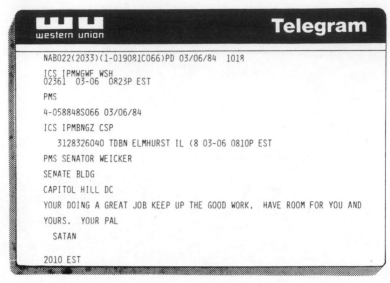

```
                                                    Telegram
western union

  NAB022(2033)(1-019081C066)PD 03/06/84   1018
  ICS IPMWGWF WSH
  02361  03-06  0823P EST
  PMS
  4-058848S066 03/06/84
  ICS IPMBNGZ CSP
      3128326040 TDBN ELMHURST IL (8 03-06 0810P EST
  PMS SENATOR WEICKER
  SENATE BLDG
  CAPITOL HILL DC
  YOUR DOING A GREAT JOB KEEP UP THE GOOD WORK.  HAVE ROOM FOR YOU AND
  YOURS.  YOUR PAL
      SATAN

  2010 EST
```

SOURCE: *Washington Post*, March 9, 1984. Reprinted by permission.

Members as a sign that they were part of the conspiracy and added their names to the list of people he attacked. From a psychological point of view, writing a member of Congress is an outlet for such people; and although these individuals are more to be pitied than censured, some congressional staff fear what such people would do if their demands were not dealt with politely. It is hard to get a feel for the generally long "kook" letters with a few excerpts, but Figures 7.13–7.21 are representative:

DARING CONGRESSIONAL RESPONSES

In most cases, members of Congress respond to even the most outrageous charges or ridiculous requests with polite self-restraint. The most common technique is to acknowledge the receipt of the letter and make some innocuous statements about appreciating the views expressed, as do the letters in Figures 7.22 and 7.23.

FIGURE 7.13

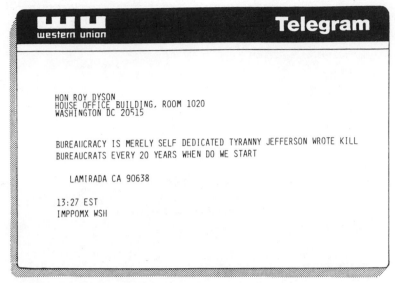

```
uu u                          Telegram
western union


HON ROY DYSON
HOUSE OFFICE BUILDING, ROOM 1020
WASHINGTON DC 20515

BUREAIICRACY IS MERELY SELF DEDICATED TYRANNY JEFFERSON WROTE KILL
BUREAUCRATS EVERY 20 YEARS WHEN DO WE START

    LAMIRADA CA 90638

13:27 EST
IMPPOMX WSH
```

SOURCE: Member's personal files.

At times the demands become so outrageous that the normal polite response seems inappropriate. Extreme frankness, or even discourtesy, tends to be the style of Members with very strong electoral bases or who are leaving the electoral arena. As a senator, John Kennedy received some rather threatening letters and responded to them by saying, "Before I turn this letter over to the FBI, I thought you would like to know that someone is writing wild and scurrilous letters over your signature." Former Ohio Senator Stephen Young, responding to a constituent complaining that he wanted his horse transported at government expense just like Caroline Kennedy's pony, retorted, "Sir: I am wondering why you need a horse when there is already one jackass at your address" (Green 1979, p. 240). The two letters in Figures 7.24 and 7.25 must stand as classics by Members fed up with constituents' mail.

Despite the previous examples, most constituents write letters which are reasonable and polite, while most offices treat the communications with the seriousness they deserve. The letters described in this chapter are the exceptions which prove the rule: funny to consider, but quite unique.

FIGURE 7.14

```
To:  Sgt. Harvey E. Looney #151        To:  F.B.I.
     Prince Georges County Police            9th & Pennsylvania Ave. N.W.
     Bowie Station                           Washington, D.C.
     601 South Crain Highway
     Upper Marlboro,
     Maryland 20870

To:  Congressman Peter W. Rodino       To:  Congressman Peter W. Rodino
     205 Crafton Ave.   (Rodino)            House of Representatives
     Newark,                                Rayburn Bldg.
     New Jersey 07104                       Room 2462
                                            Washington, D.C.
To:  Dr. Robert Schuller
     Box 100                           To:  Jim Bakker
     Garden Grove                           PTL Club
     California 82642                        Charlotte,
                                            North Carolina 28209
```

Dear Sgt. Looney, Mr. Rodino, Dr. Schuller, and Jim Bakker,

      I want to report the following concerning my problems and Gina Lollobrigida's problems.

      About two weeks ago I heard what I though were baby birds and I saw and heard two Starlings in my gutter right over the door on my back øy porch. They made a lot of noise at times and sometimes sounded like they were in the attic over my bed. Of course I knew they were not in the attic. A week later on Saturday, May 1, 10 1982, they were still building a nest with big sticks. I saw the birds with long sticks in their mouths fly up to the gutter. Some sticks had dropped on the porch and the porch was a mess with a lot of white bird droppings and they had already messed on my door which I had just cleaned for the Spring.

      All this week the birds have still been taking pieces of leaves and sticks into the gutter on the back roof over the door. These birds are working with Ø the Devil to clog my gutter and cause water to pour down over anybody going in the back door when it rains.

      Starlings have always been a nuisance. I have read where Starlings were imported to this Country from Europe around the turn of the Century (1900). In a short time they had destroyed all the Bluegirds. The Bluebird was plentiful on the East Coast before the Starlings came. The Bluebird was a Native American songbird and must have brought a little happiness to people as so many songs seem to indicated. I have never seen a Blúd Bluebird in my lifetime except in pictures. I think the Devil wanted Bluebirds destroyed.

      The Devil uses birds, animals, and insects as his eyes to see what is going on. Birds and animals I believe are really people. In one of the first Stan Laurel and Oliver Hardy movies I ever saw one of them turned into a horse and the horse talked. The Arabian Nights Movies show people being turned into dogs and horses. Ask Gina Lollobrigida, I think she can shed some light on this.

      As I have said before Doug Henning's Magic Show is sheer Witch Craft. He turns girls into animals. If this does not actd actually happen then the girls vanish to somewhere else. As the girls involved what actually happens.

SOURCE: Member's personal files.

FIGURE 7.15

```
                                        September 3, 1982

Honorable Roy Dyson
U. S. House of Representatives
Washington, DC  20515

Re:  Bishopville Post Office (21813)

Dear Mr. Dyson:

Recently the Postmaster retired.

I urge that his replacement be a Bishopville Caucasian.

                        Sincerely,


PS I'm not a candidate.
```

SOURCE: Member's personal files.

FIGURE 7.16

Dear Mr. Dyson,

I got your letter a couple day's ago. I know that crime isn't just for the poor anyone can comit a crime. Mr. Dyson, my letter isn't really about crime but I need your help in something. Why do we have to learn to park a car long way's. I think it's called parsell. Plus, there's no place to learn about parking a car. They expect you to know. I can drive a car, I just can't park, there's no place to learn. Also, maybe this question is for President Reagon, but I know you'll write back. Why must people pay taxes for everything they buy, and still pay at the end of the year?

Thank you for your time

Sincirily,

SOURCE: Member's personal files.

FIGURE 7.17

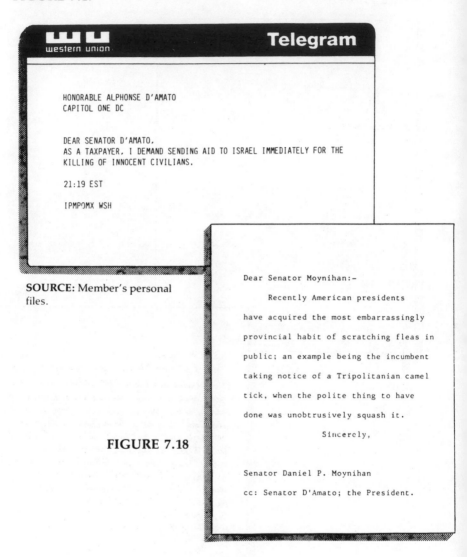

SOURCE: Member's personal files.

FIGURE 7.18

SOURCE: Member's personal files.

FIGURE 7.19

REP. DICK CHENEY

Subject: PARAQUAT — DON'T DO IT!

Date: Dec. 16, 81

GREETINGS — I RUN A SMALL BUSINESS
IN CODY (ABOUT 15 EMPLOYEES DEPENDING
ON THE SEASON), I'M IN THE 50% TAX
BRACKET, I'M AN UPSTANDING MEMBER
OF THE CODY COMMUNITY, I BELIEVE IN
THE REAGAN ECONOMIC PLAN AND FREE
ENTERPRISE IN GENERAL, I VOTED FOR
YOU LAST ELECTION, AND I SMOKE POT
IN MY LEISURE HOURS.
    FOR GODS SAKE MAN, DON'T SEND
PARAQUAT TO MEXICO. STOP THE HEROIN
& COKE, (AND THE GRASS IF YOU MUST),
BUT DON'T POISON YOUR SUPPORTERS!
(IF NOTHING ELSE, THINK OF THE MEDICAL
TREATMENT COSTS YOU'LL HAVE INCURRED!

SOURCE: Member's personal files.

FIGURE 7.20

```
Office of Hon. D'Amatto
Senate of the United States



Sir:


Please let me know if the Senator is a Democrat or a Republican.  I am
ashamed to ask my neighbors not to be ridiculed.  And if he is one or the
other, why so.


                          Sincerely,



Please don't mention this to the Senator.  People with Slavic names provide
enough amusement already.
```

SOURCE: Member's personal files.

FIGURE 7.21

SOURCE: Member's personal files.

FIGURE 7.22

Congress of the United States
House of Representatives
Washington, D.C. 20515

August 9, 1982

Mr. Prentiss N. Miles
212 Winter Quarters Drive
Pocomoke, Maryland 21851

Dear Mr. Miles:

Thank you for your letter reagrding pension reform and
H.R. 4929, the Public Employee Pension Plan Reporting and
Accountability Act. I appreciate knowing your views on this
matter.

This bill would require the full public disclosure and
reporting of information regarding state and local civil
servant retirement plans, as well as establish standards
of conduct and responsibility for trusteesof public employee
pension benefit plans. H.R. 4029 is currently awaiting action
by the House. You may be assured that I will give this measure
my close attention when it reaches the House floor and will
remain mindful of your views.

Your additional comments of this or any other matter that
may concern you are welcome. Please do not hesitate to contact
me if I may be of further service to you.

With warm regards, I am

Sincerely,

ROY DYSON
Member of Congress

SOURCE: Member's personal files.

FIGURE 7.23

Congress of the United States
House of Representatives
Washington, D.C. 20515

August 17, 1982

Colora, Maryland 21917

Dear Mr. and Mrs.

Your recent communications has been received, and
once again, I thank you for taking the time to share
your thoughts with me.

I will remain ever mindful of your comments and
try to represent you as best I can.

With kind regards, I am

Sincerely,

ROY DYSON
Member of Congress

RD:crb

SOURCE: Member's personal files.

FIGURE 7.24

Congress of the United States
House of Representatives
Washington, D.C. 20515

Mr. Robert Payne
Mt. Pleasant S.C.

Dear Mr. Paynee,

One of the benefits of leaving public office is that I no longer
have to put up with your unending drivel. I have instructed my staff to
properly dispose of any future mail from you in the only manner
appropriate to its content.

Has any of your correspondence ver shown even the common sense of a
gnat, or the simple courtesy one expects even of a small child, I would
have been more impressed with your reasoning.

Sincerely,

Mendel Davis, MC

FIGURE 7.25

Congress of the United States
House of Representatives
Washington, D.C. 20515

Dear Sir

One of the countless drawbacks of being in Congress is
that I am compelled to receive impertinent letters from
the jackass like you in which you say I promised to have
the Sierre Madre mountains reforested and I have been
in Congress two months and have not done it. Will you
please take two running jumps and go to hell.

Sincerely,

Representative John Steven McGroatarity

SOURCE: *The New York Times,* July 8, 1979, p. 20. Copyright © 1979 by The New York Times Company. Reprinted by permission.

SOURCE: Green 1979, p. 240. Reprinted by permission of Viking Penguin Inc. © 1979 by Viking Penguin Inc.

CHAPTER 8

THE POLITICAL IMPLICATIONS OF CONGRESSIONAL CORRESPONDENCE

Little systematic evidence is available on how Members' contact with their constituents influences public attitudes and votes...Incumbents have available numerous resources with which to present themselves in a favorable light to their constituents. In the absence of other communication about the incumbent, this generalized favorable image can have decisive electoral effects. (Mann 1978, pp. 72–73)

If you serve your constituents well, you serve your re-election purposes. The two can not and should not be separated...(Congressional staff member)

Both conventional wisdom and actual congressional behavior add credence to the conclusion that congressional communications efforts are important factors in determining the political support of individual Members. While Members characterize the effort they must put into the mail as everything from a "sacred opportunity" to a real "pain in the —," few Members take the risk of slacking up on their efforts. At worst, members of Congress view the mail as "a necessary evil which must be dealt with before I can get on with the bigger issues."

COMMUNICATIONS STRATEGIES AND ELECTORAL SUCCESS

One of the most widely accepted generalizations concerning members of Congress is their almost universal desire for reelection (Mayhew 1974, passim). Relatively few Members voluntarily give up their seats except in cases of incapacity or new opportunities. While voluntary departures have increased a bit in recent years, such behavior is clearly the domain of a unique minority (Frantzich 1978). The norm is for over 80 percent of any Congress to seek reelection.

Some Assumptions About Winning Congressional Elections

While winning elections still involves as much art as science, congressmen express considerable agreement over those factors that are either outside their control or do not work. Congressmen "can do little or nothing about the party division in their districts...they have little or no effect on whom the party chooses to head the ticket or once in office how that head performs" (Fiorina 1981, p. 545).

Although both party identification and citizen evaluation of the ticket deeply affect voting in congressional elections, most congressmen take these factors largely as givens which can't be changed and focus their efforts on other realms.

While democratic theory asserts that congressional elections should be referenda on the major national issues of the day, few Members of Congress act as if that were true. In the first place, congressional elections are "local, not national events" (Mann 1978, p. 1), with the perception and performance of the local candidate playing a much larger role than national issues or conditions. Secondly, most constituents know or care little about specific policy options or decisions. As one Member characterized his constituents:

> They don't know much about my votes. Most of what they know is what I tell them. They know more of what kind of guy I am. It comes through in my letters: "You care about the little guy." (Member of Congress, quoted in Fenno 1978, p. 153)

With the fixed factors beyond control and policy choices by and large irrelevant, Members work on the following assumption:

> Unless you can keep constantly in contact with your people, serving them and letting them know what you are doing, you are in a bad way. My experience is that people don't care how I vote on foreign aid, federal aid to education, and all those big issues, but they are very much interested in whether I answer their letter. (Clapp 1963, p. 58)

As another Member stated it:

> I think in my district, if I go back to the 600 people whom I've helped and they tell their kids and relatives who all live in the same district— you know, she's helped us—I'm better off. They're not going to look at my votes. I really am convinced of that. (Bibby 1983, p. 45)

The extreme emphasis congressmen put on the mail stems from the almost universal conclusions that (1) "two-way communication is more valued by their constituents than policy congruence" (Fenno 1978, p. 241) and (2) "citizen expectations of the incumbent's helpfulness are fully as important as party affiliation in their vote decisions" (Fiorina 1981, p. 561).

The Strategic Implications

The consequences of congressmen accepting the above assumptions results in the "four-P strategy" of politicizing, prioritizing, personalizing, and presenting an image though the mails.

Politicizing

Rather than viewing the demands of receiving and responding to growing mountains of mail as simply part of the job, members of Congress and their staffs view the tasks as potentially valuable political assets.

> These days , the successful politician does not see a letter from his home district as a burden, taking up valuable staff time and energy. He eagerly pounces on it as an opportunity to win another vote, to convince his constituents that, even if the government doesn't work, their representative is all right. (Feldstein 1979, p. 42)

Perquisites of offices such as the frank, free government publications, and sophisticated direct mail techniques are unabashedly used to promote reelection (Cover 1976, p. 22).

Even legitimate requests to have the congressional offices cut through bureaucratic red tape to do casework are seldom complied with out of the kindness of the Member's heart, nor are they kept on the one-to-one level. In a poll of congressional offices,

> substantial pluralities of respondents indicated that casework recipients' names were added to mailing lists; successes, at least in aggregate terms ("I helped 2500 constituents last year") are included in newsletters; and occasional cases are described in detail in campaign literature or speeches. Almost all agreed that the best dividend from casework came from word-of-mouth publicity. (Johannes 1981, p. 93)

Prioritizing

When asked what their priority in Congress was, a considerable number of congressmen echoed the member who stated:

> Staying in contact with people in my district. Answering the mail. That's
> my first priority, because it may be their only contact with the office.
> (Cavanaugh 1981, p. 66)

As Chapter 3 reveals empirically, even if the Member does not expend the majority of his effort on the mail, the efforts of the staff are
clearly concentrated in this realm. There seems to be a Gresham's Law
in most congressional offices, which results in the mail pushing aside all
other activities. The pressure of the mail (much of it self-imposed or self-
generated) impinges on everyone's work patterns. When a big mailing
is going out, the whole office, from interns to adminstrative assistants,
is likely to put aside other tasks to get the mail out. Issues, votes, and
other pressures come and go , but the continuing reality is that the mail
will always be there.

Personalizing

In an era where the individual citizen often is awed by his miniscule
proportions relative to the large and complex groups and institutions of
modern society, congressmen work hard to convey an image as a refuge from the larger pattern by treating the constituent as an individual.
By being recognized as the individual who informs constituents on issues of importance, helps them with personal problems, and deals with
them on a first-name basis, the congressman builds interpersonal ties
with political payoffs. While traveling through his district with political
scientist Richard Fenno, one congressman explained the importance of
the personal touch by saying:

> Do your remember Miss Sharp back in the post office? She had never
> met me before, but she called me Sam. That's the way the people think
> of me. No person ever voted against you if he's on a first name basis
> with you. (Fenno 1978, p. 64)

Presenting an Image

Frequent and sophisticated communication techniques count for little unless something of importance is communicated to the constituent.
The simplest purpose of communications is just to get the Member's
name out so that it will be recognized. The next step involves getting
constituents to develop a positive feeling that the Member cares about
his constituents and has served them well. If agreement on an issue is
possible, emphasize it; if disagreement remains, ignore or obfuscate. If
a constituent desires help, the ideal course is to satisfy the request; when

that remains impossible the congressmen at least want to "leave constituents thinking that they have done everything in their power to assist them" (Yiannakis 1981, p. 572). The constituent's satisfaction with the Member's efforts is as important for future voting support as solving the problem.

Actual Implications of Constituent Communications

While it is a natural desire to prove once and for all whether constituent communications strategies work or not, such a task may well be as difficult as it is unimportant. Members of Congress, as do most of us, behave on the basis of perceptions and assumptions as much as on the basis of factual truth. The fact that congressmen and their staffs believe that constituent mail is important provides as potent a stimulant to its use as an extensive collection of careful studies.

Studying the effect of the discrete set of variables associated with congressional mail strategies is fraught with many problems. Whether one is simply trying to link a particular strategy with constituent awareness or evaluation, or whether one wants to use mail strategies to predict political outcomes, only a few of the factors which may have an impact can be isolated. The importance of reelection for most Members mitigates against doing careful experiments which may affect their political future. With all these caveats in mind, some results are available.

The clearest findings result when one analyzes the opinions of constituents having unique communications linkages with a congressman's office. Individuals who recall contacting their Member's office with a casework request and getting a positive response are significantly more likely to vote for that Member, while the relatively few constituents having a negative experience are less likely to support him (Yiannakis 1981, p. 577; Fiorina 1981, p. 558). Another study points out that the positive impact may be quite temporary: "voters cannot be bought cheaply (simply by casework) or, if they can be, they do not stay bought" (Johannes and McAdams 1981, p. 539; Johannes 1984, p. 211).

Using an experimental design in one office, Al Cover was allowed to use different mailing strategies for different segments of the district and test the results. He found that initial unsolicited mailings to targeted areas increase the incumbent's name recognition and popularity significantly, while subsequent mailings have little effect (Cover 1982, p. 357).

We have considerable evidence that constituents mention district attentiveness as one of the factors they desire out of a Member (Parker 1980, p. 115), but it is unclear how this may be linked to their evaluations or votes, for broader-based studies attempting to link general communications patterns with constituent reactions have generally been less successful. In what might come as a surprise, there is a weak negative relationship between mail output and electoral security, showing that safe Members put out fewer mailings than their more electorally marginal colleagues (Cover 1976, p. 82).

This should not be surprising since safe Members may well slack off on mailings once they feel secure, whereas marginal Members look at the mail as a way to strengthen their positions and use it heavily.

While a significant amount has been written asserting the impact of congressional perquisities (especially the mail) on the electoral security of incumbents (see especially Mayhew 1974 and Fiorina 1981), some conflicting findings keep cropping up. Ferejohn (1977) found that more extensive advertising did not increase name identification. Alford argues that perquisites may not be as general an explanation for electoral advantage as is often claimed, since while both the House and Senate have had access to roughly the same increases in perquisite availability, the increase in the incumbency advantage of House members has been accompanied by a decrease in the incumbency advantage in the Senate. Either senators as a group are much less successful in using their resources, or other factors are at work (Alford 1983, p. 1).

While the empirical evidence is still out, members of Congress act as if there were no question that creating an effective two-day communications relationship with one's constituency is the key to maintaining one's political strength. "Most studies of legislators at any political level report that constituency service is perceived by legislators to be helpful to their political career" (Miller and Wrinkel 1983, p. 4).

THE CONSEQUENCES OF CONGRESSIONAL COMMUNICATIONS FOR THE POLITICAL SYSTEM

Incumbency

While we are not at the stage of being able to verify empirically that congressional mail strategies account for the increase in incumbent re-election success and the concomitant decline in close congressional contests, the consensus of observers from both the political science and journalistic realms is that there is no question about the relationship:

> The answer to the incumbency advantage question could be a remarkably simple one: the more hundreds of thousands of messages congressmen rain down on constituents, the more votes they get. (Mayhew 1974, p. 310)

The most practical advantage of incumbency, observers say, is the congressional privilege to send an almost unlimited amount of official mail by using the congressional "frank" instead of a postage stamp. (Saperstein 1982, p. a1)

There has been a substantial increase in the proportion of citizens who have written their congressman. The influx of mail has increased the opportunities for Members to serve their constituents and to publicize their attentiveness. . . . It also means that incumbents are better able to reach their constituents in a personal way (e.g. letters addressed to a specific individual rather than to "occupant"). (Parker 1980, p. 459)

For the incumbent, the most effective form of [campaign] contact is through the mails; the value of the frank is again apparent. (Jacobson 1982, p. 99)

The opportunity to do casework may well be chief among the advantages of incumbency. (Yiannakis 1981, p. 569)

While the broader implications of reelecting incumbents at a very high rate are beyond the concerns of this book, a few examples are in order. While the incumbency advantage helps assure increased continuity and experience in the Congress and may make the congressional career a more desirable one, automatically returning incumbents based on their public relations prowess does little to increase policy responsiveness and may deaden, rather than sharpen, public awareness of the broad range of political issues facing society (Mann 1978, p. 104). Recycling incumbents allows unresponsive Members to remain in office on the basis of an effective communications program well past the point that they continue to serve their constituents' views. The overwhelming experience of having incumbents almost assured of reelection discourages candidates from challenging and leads parties, volunteers, and interest groups to more readily contribute campaign sources to incumbents, which then again increases the likelihood of reelection.

Time Commitment

In an environment where time and effort are limited, the emphasis on the mail must compete with other important activities, especially a more serious analysis of policy issues:

When one asks members. . . "What are the differences between how you actually have to spend your time and what you would ideally like to do as a member of Congress?" by far the most frequent complaint, offered by 50% of the Members, is that constituent demands interfere with legislative and other activity...when asked how they reconcile these differences in their expenditure of time, Members overwhelmingly voice the sentiment that their own personal prescriptions for House activity give way to the demands of voters. (Cavanaugh 1979, p. 224)

Offices vary on the degree to which they can shelter the Member from these demands, but few offices fail to express concern about the burden of the mail on the staff.

Escalation of Demands

Constituent demands for congressional service and communications are not fixed. Working hard to handle the mail seldom means getting ahead of the game. Offices which do a good job of communicating and service find that they have developed a reputation for effectiveness and are therefore called on to do more (Powell 1982, p. i). Congressmen are willing to open this "Pandora's Box" cycle of increased effort requiring increased future effort because of the political payoffs, but many long for the earlier days when the level of expectations was lower and they did not have to keep adding new technology and gimmicks just to stay even. By painting themselves as miracle workers willing to tackle any problem and satisfy any whim, congressmen disrupt normal governmental routines and foster false expectations of what government can and should do.

Increasing Policy Leeway

If Members can divert constituent attention from the more controversial policy decisions by selectively presenting themselves and their efforts through the mail, they have more leeway to pursue legislative concerns and stands of their own choosing (Fenno 1978, p. 151; Parker 1981, p. 274). On the one hand, such leeway may be seen as denigrating the constituent-congressman representational linkage. On the other hand, it may be seen as allowing members to take some nationally oriented, statesmanlike stands instead of constantly pandering to parochial district interests. One's opinion depends on the role one thinks Congress should play.

Building Legitimacy

In a democracy, the political system needs to be perceived as legitimately contributing to most of the people's well-being in order to continue over a long period of time. People feel closer to their legislators than to any other national political figures, since legislators use their considerable resources for communications to assure constituents that they are ready and willing to listen, communicate, and serve (Loewenberg and Patterson 1979, p. 47). "There must be support of legislators, before there is support for legislatures. Eventually, support for legislators will produce support for legislatures" (Mezey 1976, pp. 124–25). Support for the legislature will then lead the way to broader support for the entire political system. The perception that constituents can always write their congressmen serves as a safety valve for both those who take advantage of the opportunity and those who do not, assuring citizens that someone out there is listening and cares. Not a minor consideration in an increasingly complex, frustrating, and anonymous world.

CONCLUSION

Congressional use of the mail is clearly a mixed bag. It facilitates the personal political goals of congressmen, while selectively increasing the knowledge of constituents and helping to solve some of their problems. Currently accepted strategies enhanced by a new technology have increased the spread and efficiency of congressional communications, while opening the door to potential negative consequences. Anyone who decries the darker side of manipulation through mail strategies cannot blame technology alone but must also jointly target the Members and the staffs who use the techniques, along with the constituents whose narrow perspectives and limited interest invite manipulation. If congressional mail existed in a vacuum with no other means for communications, both congressmen and constituents would be disadvantaged. Used as only one source of constituent information on the congressman, congressional mail provides a perspective which would be missing if citizens could rely only on the national media, the local media, or the criticisms of opponents.

CHAPTER 9

CONSTITUENT COMMUNICATIONS IN THE AGE OF MODERN INFORMATION TECHNOLOGY

Recent decades have seen dramatic changes in communications technology, and the applications to Congress's needs have not gone unheeded. As a result of the overwhelming pressure on members of Congress to develop more efficient and effective communications links with their constituents, technological changes—particularly in the areas of computerization and cable television—have opened new horizons.

> Deep down inside...every congressman believes that the correctness of his positions and votes will be evident to the electorate if only he could communicate them directly—with no 'distorting' intervention by the press. This is where the new space-age communications techniques offer some sobering possibilities. (Haskell 1982, p. 49)

THE COMPUTERIZATION OF CONGRESSIONAL MAIL

> We are in the new era of machine politics, where the machine is the computer. (Alan Baron, quoted in Green 1979, p. 276)

During the last decade, Congress has gone from the backwaters of computerization to the forefront. While many of Congress's chosen applications have an impact on organizational efficiency and information retrieval, the use of computers in individual congressional offices is dominated by constituent communications applications (see Table 9.1).

The House and Senate approached computerization of mail in two very different ways. In the House, individual Member offices chose to

TABLE 9.1

COMPUTER USES IN THE HOUSE OF REPRESENTATIVES
(percentage using computers for designated functions in 1977)

Correspondence Management		59
Mail production	29	
Labels	11	
Mailing lists	30	
Targeted mail	23	
Newsletters	15	
Mail counts	8	
Information Retrieval		29
Office Administration and Supervision		23

NOTE: Multiple responses account for totals equalling more than 100 percent.
SOURCE: U.S., Congress, House, Commission on Administrative Review 1977, p. 1072.

use office funds for contracting with outside vendors or establishing their own individual in-house word processing and mailing list capabilities. The acceptance of computerization was largely generational and political, with Members familiar with computers from outside contact or in need of bolstering their electoral bases seeking out computer applications first. More politically secure Members and those fully satisfied with their existing methods of handling correspondence lagged behind, expressing fears that constituents would not want to be treated like numbers (Kroger 1978, p. 37) and bewailing the increased cost of computerization. Within ten years of the initial computer applications in 1974, virtually every House office used computers to some degree. In the Senate, a centralized Correspondence Management System (CMS) became available to all Members in 1980. The CMS allows offices to create and manage targeted mailing lists which can be used to send out newsletters and more personalized mail. In 1984, the Senate began to move toward a massive influx of micro-computers to augment the centralized system. (For a fuller description of the adoption process, see Frantzich 1982, Chapter 4.)

Computerized Mail Applications

In most cases, the introduction of the computer into congressional offices did not change basic communications strategies as much as it increased efficiency and made possible approaches which in the past could be used only with great expenditure of time and effort.

Mail Monitoring

While most offices keep mail counts on letters received on key issues, logging incoming mail into the computer gives Members with such a capability not only the raw figures of support and opposition, but also a feeling for the kinds of individuals taking various stands. As one staff member put it, "In the past we used to weigh the mail. Now we have accurate mail counts from the computer." The computer is just beginning to be used to help Members develop and analyze their poll results in a more reliable manner. Such developments, properly used, could well help make constituent views more accessible to their congressmen.

Targeted Mail

While targeting specific messages to identifiable constituents has long been common practice, it was not until the arrival of the computer that such techniques could be used on a large scale. Traditionally, congressional offices filed the hard copy of a constituent letter on the basis of one criterion (date of arrival, constituent name, subject matter, etc.). Physically sorting such letters on the basis of other criteria represented a Herculean job which was seldom attempted. With a computer filing system, incoming mail gets cross-referenced by an almost unlimited number of categories, and mailing lists can be created directly.

While mailing lists were common in the precomputer age, the bulky and inefficient addressograph plates were time consuming to create and use, and allowed little more than producing rather smudgy copies of an entire list. One of the main reasons the Senate went to computerization was that the heavy addressograph plates were beginning to buckle the floor of the storage areas. Hard copy mailing lists had to be duplicated for each mailing, and it was almost impossible to share lists and purge them of duplicates outside of a very labor-intensive (and expensive) human process.

> Before computers, a legislator had a difficult time keeping up with incoming mail and little opportunity to develop his or her own mailing list beyond those constituents who contacted their representative. (Pincus 1977c, p. a2)

With computers, the time and resources once devoted to getting a useful list are now spent on tailoring lists to specific needs and developing the appropriate communications content.

Personalizing and Targeting Content

One of the guiding assumptions of modern mailing techniques is that individuals want to be treated as individuals. In the not-so-distant past, mass mailings looked like mass mailings, rather than having that personalized "IBM Selectric" look which implies that someone cared enough to send you an important letter, not just another piece of junk mail. Computer-based typewriters that merge recipient files for personalized salutations, addresses, and name mentioning in the text (such as the famous Publisher's Clearing House ads) imply personalization and make the letter more inviting to open and read. New jet ink and laser printers increase the creation speed without much loss of quality, with some machines printing over 15,000 "personal" letters per day (Burnham 1980, p. 96).

Just as important as having the letter look right is having it say the right thing. Increasingly, congressional offices have been developing banks of interchangeable paragraphs which can be used over and over to tailor just the right letter to an individual. Even as early as 1979, a top staff member estimated that 60–80 percent of all Senate mail comes from prepared texts. While one can rightfully argue that telling the constituent what he wants to hear distorts the representational process, there is some corrective in the fear Members have of getting caught saying two different things. There is also the positive factor that knowing a paragraph will be used many times encourages Members and their staffs to carefully frame it in a way which truly represents the Members' thinking. Thus, computerization may well increase the frequency, efficiency, and quality of information received by a constituent.

Computers and Casework

Computers also find effective usage in monitoring and performing constituent casework. In some offices, incoming casework letters are put into a computerized "action file" with a "tickler" system. Careful records are kept of the actions taken on each case, with specific dates indicated to remind ("tickle") the caseworker to check on the progress. Some offices are communicating with bureaucratic offices using electronic mail, thus increasing the speed and efficiency of intervening with the bureaucracy for a constituent.

Implications of Computerized Mail

Computerizing a congressional office's mailings undoubtedly increases efficiency in dealing with a particular letter, but the broader implications of applying this new technology are not simply analogous to moving from a manual to an electric typewriter. Computerization is not simply a change in the *degree* of efficiency, but carries with it changes in the *kind* of things congressmen can and must do. The availability of the computer almost demands its use. The "law of the instrument" (give a child a hammer and the whole world becomes a nail) applies (Kaplan 1964, p. 28). Congressional offices have used computerized mailing capabilities not only to react to outside demands, but also for sophisticated outreach programs which increase the incoming mail. Rather than technology helping them get ahead of the game, it has spawned new demands, and offices still struggle to keep their heads above water.

In a broader realm, computerized mail increases the spread of impact so greatly that it puts the electoral challenger at just that much more of a disadvantage in competing with the incumbent, whose government-subsidized computer-mailing capabilities have numerous direct and indirect electioneering possibilities.

THE CUTTING EDGE OF THE FUTURE

While the above applications are both readily available and commonly used, a number of other advances in communications technology remain primarily in the experimental stages, and the potential uses and implications are more speculative.

Congressional Monitoring Through Cable Television

Since 1979, when the House of Representatives first allowed cameras into the chamber to broadcast proceedings live, constituents with cable access have had a new method of monitoring the Congress, and Members have found a potent new method of communicating. Today over 18 million households have access to C–SPAN, the Cable Satellite Public Affairs Network. While C–SPAN viewers number relatively few constituents, they tend to be interested, articulate, and overrepresentative of the kinds of participatory citizens to whom congressmen must be most attentive. Members and their staffs report a new phenomenon of constituents monitoring C–SPAN and then making timely demands for action.

> The woman on the phone that afternoon urged me to "tell the congressman to vote for what they are talking about right now on the television." (Haskell 1982, p. 48)

By upgrading a select group of constituents' direct access to congressional proceedings without the distortions of the press, interest groups, or the self-serving selectivity of the Members, cable television may well enhance citizen competency:

> Broadcasting of Congressional sessions apparently has reduced the power of lobbyists, who now have competition in their efforts to convince the public of the rightness of their views. Interested observers are tuning in to congressional sessions and realizing that many issues are

far more complex than lobbyists had led them to believe. (Graber 1980, p. 210)

Realizing the potential of direct access to congressional news, Congress as an institution did all in its power to shape the kind of coverage presented. Rejecting open access to the floor by commercial broadcasters, the House retained control of the cameras and limited coverage to fixed cameras focused on only the person holding the floor (see Frantzich 1982b for more details on the adoption process). While this gives a more sanitized image by avoiding broadcasting embarrassing pictures of a few members in an almost empty chamber, or of those present not paying attention, C–SPAN viewers still have much more access than citizens in the past.

Individual members have shown considerable creativity in using C–SPAN to communicate with their constituents. The increased numbers of one-minute speeches at the beginning of each session and speeches during the "Special Orders" period at the end of the day are commonly constituency-oriented. Some Members increase the constituency viewership by giving them a "heads up" as to when their Member will be speaking.

Other Members have experimented with video-conferencing via satellite. The Member arranges to speak with a school class, civic group, or the like and responds to its questions or suggestions (Wood et al., 1979). Such a system not only allows more efficient use of the Member's time by reducing travel, but also allows targeting a message and providing for constituent involvement.

Electronic Mail

Traditional methods of mailing hard copies of documents are slow, but using the telephone can be inefficient as individuals play "telephone tag," trying to catch each other in. Communicating through computer terminals avoids both of these problems, since "mail" can be sent instantaneously 24 hours a day and reviewed at the recipient's convenience. Although most congressional offices have access to electronic mail for communications with each other, district offices, and selected segments of the bureaucracy, the impact on constituency communications has been only marginal so far. Electronic mail allows congressional offices to decentralize and handle more of their casework functions in district offices. It also allows offices to send texts of general letters for printing and distribution from district offices, thus cutting a number of days off normal mail delivery. Some offices report that the bureaucracy responds more quickly and positively to casework requests which are sent via electronic mail, since less effort is required.

The direct use of electronic mail for constituency communications remains in its infancy. A small number of House offices comprised a pilot project which allowed constituents with home computers to dial into an "electronic mailbox" and leave their message. Offices in the pilot project indicate that the use was slow to catch on:

> Our first communications came from computer types who had picked up the story through the media. They were quite excited and simply "wrote" to say "congrats." Now we are getting the more typical communications from people who want to express opinions, students who need help with projects, and general casework.

Initial electronic communications were only one-way, since each constituent would have to have an electronic mailbox to receive messages.

Since initial constituent usage was quite limited, this application is currently on hold until electronic mail becomes more widely used among the public. But the potential is there.

The spread of electronic mail portends some dramatic implications. Combined with up-to-date information on upcoming decisions through C–SPAN or some other method, electronic mail reduces the timeliness problem that occurs when constituent communications arrive after decisions are made. It is not too far-fetched to imagine a cadre of political activists monitoring deliberations on C–SPAN and zapping in their voting preferences just as the vote begins. A number of interest groups have been polling their membership and noting home computer ownership so they can be the first out of the starting blocks in using electronic mail for their causes. The speed and ease of electronic mail could give new meaning to citizen access. As one congressman predicted:

> Soon a person will be sitting home watching 60 Minutes and he'll see Mike Wallace do an expose on high taxes and he'll say "Damn it, I want to balance the budget," so he'll flip a switch on the back of his television and plug in a phone line and away you go with a message [to a congressman] that says, "I just saw on 60 Minutes how much money we're wasting on such and such a program and I want you to know how angry I am." It would make the country more democratic. (Miller 1983, pp. 20–21)

Teledemocracy

There is no reason to assume that citizens could only react to past political events. Electronic mail provides the opportunity for participatory democracy through instant plebiscites;

> The citizens...would be able to tune in on the highest level discussion of the big issues and take part by expressing their opinions electroni-

cally from their houses in the deliberations of Congress. (Adams and
Hayden 1973, p. 397)

Proponents of such a system envision the priming of the electorate
through televised discussions and debates followed by simultaneous voting via special television set home computer adapters. Following the
vote, Congress would deal with the recommendation as it would a proposal from a committee. A prototype of such a system, QUBE, is operational through cable television in Columbus, Ohio and has been used
to assess political preferences (Lauden 1977, p. 28).

As one might expect, evaluations of such a system are split. The
proponents portend a more informed public, better policy decisions, and
a renewal of democracy. Opponents point out that the elite would still
control the priming of issues during the debate period (Lauden 1977, p.
31) and would probably tend to oversimplify important issues and
manipulate the information presented (McHale 1976, p. 80). There are
also fears that a computerized plebiscite would reduce the time for careful
consideration and coalition building and increase the level of conflict.
While Marshall McLuhan argues that "instant information creates involvement," such involvement would reduce the tempering role of
Congress.

> Such instant communication with congressmen will be volatile because
> the normal cooling-off time it used to take to send a letter or even a tel-
> egram will dissappear. "Electronic mob rule," says Kenneth Showalter,
> former staff director of the House Policy Group on Information and
> Computers. "If congressmen are to be the lightning rods of public opin-
> ion, let's hope to God there's a fuse on the end of it." (Miller 1983,
> p. 21)

Unless someone made sure that everyone had access and the facility to communicate electronically, there would be no assurance that communications would be any more representative than under the current
system. Without guarantees of universal access, such a system would
contribute to a new power-and-information underclass whose financial
resources do not allow it to have the technology and whose lack of abil-
ities would make it impossible to "play the game" (Porat 1978,
pp. 41–44):

> This, like other high-tech innovations, raises the question of whether
> the new direct communications with representatives will give affluent
> citizens, who can afford home computers and cable television subscrip-
> tions, more voice in government than those in lower income brackets.
> (Haskell 1982, p. 49)

Even if we could solve all the access problems, the desirability of direct citizen access remains a question. In Herbert Simon's words, ''The genius of Democratic government is not arithmetic; it is informed consensus. . . The most positive contribution of the computer lies in informing the public, not in counting noses'' (Simon 1975, p. 224).

Fears and implications notwithstanding, the adoption of technology tends to take on a life of its own. In a realm charged by the desire to secure one's political power and satisfy policy goals, the gaining of political advantage—no matter how momentary—through the application of new technology often overshadows the warnings of naysayers predicting dire long-term consequences.

It is safe to say that in the future much of the debate over congressional-constituent communications will involve the appropriateness of the technology as much as the substance of the communications.

CHAPTER 10

"WRITE YOUR CONGRESSMAN":
Does the Advice
Still Make Sense?

If you could get two or three thousand of your closest personal friends to write well-documented letters expressing the same basic thrust to one member of Congress in a timely and efficient manner, there would be little question about your high potential for changing his policy decision or taking care of your individual casework request. For most citizens, though, the operative question is whether their individual efforts to inform or request something of their own congressmen is worth it. A few generalizations initially define the answer. Individual casework requests are likely to have more of an impact than attempts to affect the course of policy decisions. By its very nature, a casework request demands a personal response and is unlikely to be the subject of great conflict. For the congressional office, casework is almost pure profit with relatively low cost. In the policy realm, the individual citizen must compete with a panoply of other requestors whose communications volume and skills may well overwhelm the lone letter. Unless you are communicating on a topic of very limited interest to others and of little concern to the Member, every attempt must be made to make sure your letter is heard.

INCREASING ONE'S CHANCES OF IMPACT

Targeting

Whom you write when dealing with Congress may be just as important as what you write. Members of Congress think in terms of their responsibility to individuals residing in geographic districts. Unless you can make a case that you have a right to inform particular committee members before a decision by the entire chamber, letters to anyone but your own representative or senators are likely to be "bucked" back to one of them anyway. If you have had some personal contact with one of your Members, that is the first place to start:

> While it certainly cannot hurt to refer in your letter to personal friendship, acquaintanceship or specific time and place of meeting with the Congressman, fabricating or embellishing your relationship with the Congressman is of no consequence.(Butler et al. 1983, p. 1)

Members entering Congress with relatively weak electoral margins tend to develop responsive communications patterns that they maintain over time, and they would be good targets. For casework requests, you will have more success if one of your Members is on the committee overseeing the agency in question or if he is a Member of the president's party. Responsiveness may be a bit greater when a Member is running for reelection.

Format

Members of Congress evaluate the effort involved in a communication as a surrogate measure of the veracity of the request. Personal letters carry significantly more weight than form letters, telegrams, or phone calls.

In a setting dominated by information overload, brevity is important. A short and to-the-point letter (not over two pages) has a much better chance of being digested and acted upon than a lengthy and rambling tome (DeKiefper 1981, p. 57).

Timing

As with most things in life, timing of communications is crucial. Complicated casework requests arriving at the last minute have a good chance of being ignored. The problem is even more evident when dealing with issue mail. The policymaking process in Congress involves a number of decision-making stages. Those communications reaching a member before he must make a public commitment are much more potent than the more typical letter which reacts to press reports of a decision already made. In some cases past decisions cannot be revised. In any case, politicians, while intellectually believing Emerson's view that "consistency is the hobgoblin of little minds," realize that in politics it is usually better to be consistently wrong in some people's minds than to be seen as inconsistent. For the individual citizen, monitoring the congressional process in such a way as to anticipate upcoming decisions offers a significant challenge.

While most congressional offices respond to every letter, communications do "fall through the cracks" or get caught in the backlog. If you have heard nothing for three or four weeks, a follow-up letter is certainly in order. Refer to the first letter and indicate how anxious you are to get a reply (DeKiefper 1981, pp. 67–69).

What to Communicate

Personalization

Members of Congress generally know the basic issues and the legislative intent behind bureaucratic rules which may lead to casework demands. Unless a constituent is a substantive expert, his chief contribution lies in outlining how a particular policy affects his life. The most useful communications are "first person factual accounts of a constituent's own personal experiences" (Miller 1962, p. 72). As Congressman Morris Udall put it:

> Form letters often receive form replies. . . . I usually know what the major lobbying groups are saying, but I don't often know of YOUR experiences and observations, or what the proposed bill will do to and for you. (Udall 1967, p. 2)

In terms of casework, congressmen see themselves as conduits for individual citizens desiring to solve problems on their own. Most offices will not take casework requests from constituents represented by a lawyer, since they feel that "the lawyer is getting paid for his representation and can do the work himself" (Cohen and Lasson 1982, p. 15).

Knowledge

Constituents who demonstrate a familiarity with the Member, the issue, and the nature of the legislative process have an advantage over their less-informed neighbors. The letter which subtly lets the congressman know that the writer has an issue preference and will be watching has more impact than the emotional tirade and not-so-cloaked threat:

> Many people who write their congressman tend to be more opinionated than informed. They are entitled to their opinions, of course, but when it comes to influencing me, the soundness of their logic, rather than the heights of their emotion or the depths of their conviction is much more

likely to carry the day (Congressman James Quigley, [D–PA], quoted in Davis 1961, p. 21)

Specificity

Vague requests to "reduce the rate of inflation" or "stop nuclear proliferation" lead to vague letters of response rather than thoughtful consideration. Specific requests to act in a particular way on a specific bill put the demand in a format of required decision, with which all members of Congress are familiar, if not comfortable. The citizen with a specific complaint about impending legislation is likely to have more success by requesting specific action on an amendment, rather than forcing a member to oppose the whole package. Congressman Udall pleads with constituents not to "demand a commitment before the facts are in," to be constructive by not berating individuals with whom they have honest disagreements, and to encourage responsiveness by telling the congressman of a "job well done" when such commendation is deserved (Udall 1967, pp. 2–3).

Some Special Hints for Casework Requests

Asking an office to do casework requires imparting very specific information. Senator William Cohen (Cohen & Lasson, 1982 passim) makes the following suggestions:

DO include all relevant identifying information, such as your name, address, telephone numbers, and places where you can be reached away from home or office.
DO describe your problem clearly, concisely, and candidly.
DO outline the steps you have taken so far to solve the problem.
DON'T misrepresent or conceal any relevant facts.
DON'T suggest that your political support for the congressman or senator you are contacting is contingent upon his solving your problem.
DON'T write more than one congressman or senator about the same problem.
DON'T wait until the last minute if it is clear that solving your problem will take some time.

Joining Forces

In a political system based on majority rule, numbers often play more of a role than the nature of the communicators or the quality of their communications. "Collectively, citizens have a greater impact when initiating contacts with public officials than when acting individually"

(Meadow 1980, p. 77). Before firing off even the most well-crafted letter, the interested constituent would be well advised to determine the availability of individuals or groups willing to join in the effort. A few letters can be written off as the work of "the lunatic fringe," while a few dozen letters are harder to rationalize away. If your argument is good enough that you think you can sway a member of Congress, it should be good enough to sway a group of fellow citizens first.

CONCLUSION

The two-way communications between citizens and members of Congress serves as an important link in the representative process. The recent dramatic increase in both incoming and outgoing mail should be viewed with more appreciation than alarm. While the previous pages have chronicled examples of undesirable manipulation of government by citizens and of misleading of constituents by congressional offices, both sides of the communications equation are better informed than they would be without communications. Like all tools, the mail can be used appropriately or inappropriately. The proper response is not to condemn the mail, but to educate its users and enhance the defenses of its recipients.

The previous pages may well have put the individual citizen in a quandary. No aware citizen can believe that an individual letter will be carefully read by a member of Congress and be both the highlight of the day and the primary factor in a major policy decision. On the other hand, one letter can have and has had considerable impact on the course of government. No one wants to feed a system which smacks of self-serving manipulation, but interested citizens who sit back and refuse to participate because the constituent-congressional communications interchange is imperfect are missing the point. The task lies in improving the communications link, not breaking it. The citizen with a legitimate interest in communicating with a member of Congress may not succeed in every case, but a communication which is never even attempted unquestionably will not have the desired impact.

BIBLIOGRAPHY

Adams, J. Mack, and Douglas H. Hayden. 1973. *Computers: Appreciation, Applications, Implications.* New York: John Wiley and Sons.

Alford, John R. 1983. "Incumbency Advantage in Senate Elections." Paper presented at the 1983 convention of the Midwest Political Science Association.

American Historical Review. 1979. "Circular Letters of Congressmen to Their Constituents, 1789–1829." *American Historical Review* v. 84 (June): p. 847.

Anagnosen, J. Theodore. 1982. "The Electoral Impact of Constituency Aggressiveness." Unpublished paper.

Anderson, Gary. 1983. "Political Action Committees: Attaining Technical Sophistication." *Campaigns and Elections* 4 (Summer):25–30.

Arieff, Irwin B. 1979. "Computers and Direct Mail Are Being Married on the Hill to Keep Incumbents in Office." *Congressional Quarterly Weekly Report* 37 (July 21):445–48.

——. 1982. "High Cost Estimates Threaten Senator's New Mail Privilege." *Congressional Quarterly Weekly Report* 40 (February 6):206.

Barker, Karyn. 1983. "Hill's Paper Tiger Has a Voracious Appetite." *Washington Post*, May 8, 1983:A1.

Bibby, John. 1983. *Congress Off the Record.* Washington, D.C: American Enterprise Institute.

Bond, Jon R. 1983. "Dimensions of District Attention over Time." Paper presented at the 1983 convention of the Midwest Political Science Association.

Born, Richard. 1982. "Perquisite Employment in the U.S. House of Representatives, 1960–1976: The Influence of Generational Change." *American Politics Quarterly* 10 (July):347–62.

Breslin, Janet. 1977. "Constituent Service." In U.S., Congress, Senate. Commission on the Operation of the Senate. *Senators: Office Ethics and Pressures.* 94th Congress, 1st Session, Committee Print: Washington D.C.: Government Printing Office. 19–36.

Burnham, David. 1980. "Congress' Computer Subsidy." *New York Times Magazine* November 2, 1980, p. 96.

Butler, Peter B., Vickie Smith and Gloria Van Treese. 1983. *Dear Congressman: Help.* Tallahassee, Fla.: Stone House.

Carlile, Judy. 1981a. *A Functional Analysis of Congressional Member Office Operations.* Congressional Research Service Report no. 81-116. Washington, D.C.: Government Printing Office.

——. 1981b. *Casework in a Congressional Office.* Congressional Research Service Report no. 81-46. Washington, D.C.: Government Printing Office.

Cavanaugh, Thomas E. 1979. "The Rational Allocation of Congressional Resources: Member Time and Staff Use in the House." In *Public Policy and*

Public Choice, edited by Douglas Rae and Theodore Eismeier. pp. 209–47. Beverly Hills, Calif.: Sage.

———. 1981. "The Two Arenas of Congress." In *Congress at Work,* edited by Joseph Cooper and G. C. Mackenzie, pp. 56–77. Austin, Tex.: University of Texas Press.

Clapp, Charles. 1963. *The Congressman: His Work as He Sees It.* Washington, D.C.: The Brookings Institution.

Clark, Joseph. 1964. *Congress: The Sapless Branch.* Westport, Conn.: Greenwood Press.

Cnudde, Charles F. and Donald J. McCrone. 1966. "The Linkage between Constituency Attitudes and Congressional Voting Behavior: A Causal Model." *American Political Science Review* 60 (March):66–72.

Common Cause. 1981. Plaintiff's motion for summary judgement, *"Common Cause vs. Bolger,"* Civil Action 1887-73.

Cohen, William S. and Kenneth Lasson. 1982. *Getting the Most out of Washington.* New York: Facts on File.

Congressional Quarterly. 1974. "The Impeachment Lobby: Emphasis on Grass Roots Pressure," *Congressional Quarterly Weekly Report* 32 (May 25):1368–74.

———. 1976. *Guide to the U.S. Congress.* Washington, D.C.: Congressional Quarterly Press.

———. 1979. *Guide to the U.S. Congress,* 2 ed. Washington, D.C.: Congressional Quarterly Press.

Cover, Albert. 1976. "One Good Term Deserves Another: The Advantage of Incumbency in Congressional Elections." Paper presented at the 1976 meeting of the American Political Science Association.

———. 1980. "Contacting Congressional Constituents: Some Patterns of Perquisite Use." *American Journal of Political Science* 24 (February):125–35.

———. and Bruce Brumberg. 1982. "Baby Books and Ballots: The Impact of Congressional Mail on Constituent Opinion." *American Political Science Review* 76 (June):347–59.

Cranor, John D. and Joseph W. Westphal. 1978. "Congressional District Offices, Federal Programs and Electoral Benefits." Paper presented at the 1978 meeting of the Midwest Political Science Association.

Cranston, Alan. 1975. "Comments on Casework." 89th Congress, 1st Session: S17853-17854. *Congressional Record.*

Crick, Bernard. 1965. *The Reform of Parliament.* New York: Anchor Books.

Cunningham, Noble E. 1978. *Circular Letters of Congressmen to Their Constituents 1789–1829.* Chapel Hill: University of North Carolina Press.

Davidson, Roger H. 1966. "Congress and the Executive: The Race for Representation." In *Congress: The First Branch of Government,* edited by Edward deGrazia, pp. 377–414. Washington, D.C.: American Enterprise Institute.

———. and Walter J. Oleszek. 1981. *Congress and Its Members.* Washington, D.C.: Congressional Quarterly Press.

Davis, Ellen. 1961. "Don't Write Your Congressman Unless..." *Harpers* 12 (June):10.

deGrazia, Edward, ed. 1966. *Congress: The First Branch of Government.* Washington, D.C.: American Enterprise Institute.

Dekieffer Donald. 1981. *How to Lobby Congress.* New York: Dodd and Mead.

Dertouzos, Michael L. and Joel Moses, eds. 1975. *The Computer Age: A Twenty Year View.* Cambridge, Mass. Massachusetts Institute of Technology Press.

Dexter, Lewis A. 1956. "What Do Congressmen Hear: The Mail. *"Public Opinion Quarterly* 20 (Spring): 16.

Dodd, Lawrence and Richard Schott. 1979. *Congress and the Administrative State.* New York: John Wiley and Sons.

Edsall, Thomas B. 1983. "House Votes to Repeal Witholding." *Washington Post,* May 18, 1983, p. al.

Ehrenhart, Alan. 1982. "Incumbency Insurance: The Extended Frank." *Congressional Quarterly Weekly Report* 40 (June 19):1499.

Erickson, Robert S. 1978. "Constituency Opinion and Congressional Behavior: A Reexamination of the Miller-Stokes Representation Data," *American Journal of Political Science* 22 (August):511–35.

——. and Gerald C. Wright Jr. 1980. "Policy Representation of Constituency Interests." *Political Behavior* 2:91–106.

Eulau, Heinz. 1967. "Changing Views of Representation." In *Contemporary Political Science,* edited by Ithiel de Sola Pool, pp. 53–85. New York: McGraw Hill.

——. and Paul D. Karps. 1977. "The Puzzle of Representation: Specifying Components of Responsiveness." *Legislative Studies Quarterly* 2 (August):233–54.

Evins, Joe. 1963. *Understanding Congress.* New York: Clarkson N. Potter.

Feldstein, Mark. (1979). "Mail Fraud of Capitol Hill." *Washington Monthly* 1 (October):41–48.

Fenno, Richard F. 1977. "U.S. House Members in Their Constituencies." *American Political Science Review* 77 (Spring):883–917.

——. 1978. *Home Style: House Members in Their Districts.* Boston: Little Brown.

Ferejohn, John. 1974. *Pork Barrel Politics.* Stanford, Calif.: Stanford University Press.

Fiorina, Morris. 1977. Congress: *The Keystone of the Washington Establishment.* New Haven: Yale University Press.

Flerage, Ellen. 1975. "Representational Quality: What Difference Does Voting Make?" Paper presented at the 1975 meeting of the Midwest Political Science Association.

Fox, Harrison and Susan Webb Hammond. 1977. *Congressional Staffs.* New York: The Free Press.

Frantzich, Stephen E. 1978. "De-recruitment; The Other Side of the Congressional Career Equation," *Western Political Quarterly* (March): 105–26.

——. 1982a. *Computers in Congress: The Politics of Information.* Beverly Hills, Calif. Sage Publications.

——. 1982b. "Communications and Congress," In *The Communications Revolution in Politics*, edited by Gerald Benjamin, pp. 88–101. New York: Academy of Political Science.

Fulbright, J. William. 1979. "The Legislator as Educator." *Foreign Affairs* 57 (Spring):719–32.

Gellhorn, Walter. 1966. *When Americans Complain*. Cambridge, Mass.: Harvard University Press.

Graber, Doris A. 1980. *Mass Media and American Politics* . Washington, D.C.: Congressional Quarterly Press.

Green, Mark. 1979. *Who Runs Congress?* New York: Bantam Books.

Hammond, Susan Webb. 1981. "Management of Legislative Offices. In *The House at Work*, edited by Joseph C. Cooper and G. Calvin Mackenzie, pp 183–209. Houston: University of Texas Press.

Haskell, Anne. 1982. "Live from Capitol Hill: Where Politicians Use High Technology to Bypass the Press." *Washington Journalism Review* 4 (November):48–50.

Haydon, William. 1980. Confessions of a High-tech Politico: Mr. Wang Goes to Washington." *Washington Monthly* 12 (May):43–48.

Himowitz, Michael J. 1982. "Senator's Postage Bill Spurs Hearings," *Baltimore Evening Sun*, September 13, 1982.

Hinckley, Barbara. 1978. *Stability and Change in Congress*. New York: Harper and Row.

Hurley, Patricia A. and Kim Quaile Hill. 1980. "The Prospects for Issue Voting in Contemporary Congressional Elections." *American Politics Quarterly* 8 (October):425–48.

Jacobson, Gary C. 1983. *The Politics of Congressional Elections*. Boston: Little Brown.

Johannes, John R. 1980. "The Distribution of Casework in the U.S. Congress." *Legislative Studies Quarterly* 5 (November):517–44.

——. 1981. "Casework in the House." In *The House at Work*, edited by Joseph Cooper and G. C. Mackenzie, pp. 78–96. Houston: University of Texas Press.

——. 1984. *To Serve the People: Congress and Constituency Service*. Lincoln, Neb. University of Nebraska Press.

——. and John C. McAdams. 1981. "The Congressional Incumbency Effect: Is It Casework, Policy Compatibility or Something Else?" *American Journal of Political Science* 25 (August):pp. 512–42.

——. and John C. McAdams. 1983. "Congressmen and Constituents: A Panel Study, 1977–1982." Paper presented at the 1983 meeting of the American Political Science Association.

Johnson, Kathryn. 1981. "What Lawmakers Must Do for the Folks Back Home." *U.S. News and World Report*, March 2, 1981, pp. 39–40.

Jost, Steve. 1979. "The Automated Congressional Office." *Data Management* 17 (May):46–50.

Kaplan, A. 1964. *The Conduct of Inquiry*. San Francisco: Chandler.

Keller, Bill. 1982. "Computers and Laser Printers have Recast the Injunction 'Write Your Congressman'." *Congressional Quarterly Weekly Report* 40 (September 11):225–47.

Kennedy, Cornelius B. 1980. "Time to Re-examine the 'Legislative Function' of Congress," *American Bar Association Journal* 66 (June):730–33.

Kingdon, John W. 1981. *Congressmen's Voting Decisions*. New York: Harper and Row.

Kravitz, Walter. 1972. *Casework by Members of Congress: A Survey of the Literature*. Congressional Research Service Report no. 72-2546612. Washington, D.C.: Government Printing Office.

Kroger, William. 1978. "How Congressmen Respond to Mountains of Mail." *Nation's Business* 66 (May):36–38.

Lane, Robert E. 1962. *Political Ideology*. New York: Free Press.

Lauden, Kenneth C. 1977. *Communications Technology and Democratic Participation*. New York: Praeger.

Light, Larry. 1981. "Crack 'Outreach' Programs No Longer Ensure Re-election." *Congressional Quarterly Weekly Report* 39 (February 14):316–18.

Lightman, David. 1979. "Our Million Dollar Congressmen." *Baltimore Sun*, September 28:A7, A4.

Loewenberg, Gerhard and Samuel Patterson. 1979. *Comparing Legislatures*. Boston: Little Brown.

Lowell, Juliet. 1960. *Dear Mr. Congressman*. New York: Duell, Sloan, and Pearce.

Long, Clarence. 1964. *Congressional Record*:21480, 88th Cong. 2nd Session, vol. 110 number 116.

Mann, Thomas E. 1978. *Unsafe at Any Margin*. Washington, D.C.: American Enterprise Institute.

Maskell, Jack. 1981. *Summary of Guidelines for Congressional Franking*. Congressional Research Service Report no. 81-271a. Washington, D.C.: Government Printing Office.

Mathias, Charles (1982a) "Congressional Mass Mailing." *Congressional Record*, 97th Cong. 2nd Session, vol. 128, no. 120.

——. 1982b. "Senatorial newsletters." *Congressional Record*, 97th Cong., 2nd Session, vol. 128, no. 153.

Matthews, Donald. 1960 *U.S. Senators and Their World*. Chapel Hill: University of North Carolina Press.

Mayhew, David R. 1974. *Congress: The Electoral Connection*. New Haven: Yale University Press.

McCloskey, Paul N. 1972. *Truth and Untruth*. New York: Simon and Schuster.

McHale, John. 1976. *The Changing Information Environment*. Denver: Westview Press.

Meadow, Robert G. 1980. *Politics as Communication*. Norwood, N.J.: Ablex Publishing Corporation.

Mezey, Michael L. 1976. "Constituency Demands and Legislative Support: An Experiment." *Legislative Studies Quarterly* 1 (February):101–28.

Miller, Clem. 1962. *Member of the House*. New York: Scribner's.

Miller, Lawrence W. and Robert D. Wrinkle. 1983. "Errand-boy or Constituency Service: A Multi-state Study of Municipal legislators." Paper presented at the 1983 meeting of the Midwest Political Science Association.

Miller, Tim. 1983. "Why Congress Wants Computers." *Washington Post*, May 15, 1983, pp. a20–a21.

Miller, Warren and Donald E. Stokes. 1963. "Constituency Influence in Congress." *American Political Science Review* 57 (March):55.

Moynihan, Elizabeth B. 1981. "Mail Call on Capitol Hill." *New York Times Magazine* November 15, 1981, pp. 136–39, 151, 158, 164–65.

O'Donnell, Thomas. 1980. "A Study of the Information Requirements of Members' Offices." Member Services Division, House Information System. Unpublished.

Ogul, Morris. 1976. *Congress Oversees the Bureaucracy.* Pittsburgh Pa.: Pittsburgh University Press.

Olson, Kenneth G. 1966. "The Service Function of the U.S. Congress." In *Congress: The First Branch of Government,* edited by Alfred de Grazia, pp. 337–76. Washington, D.C.: American Enterprise Institute.

Ornstein, Norman, Thomas S. Mann, Michael Malbin, Allen Schick, and John F. Bibby. 1982. *Vital Statistics on the U.S. Congress, 1982.* Washington, D.C.: American Enterprise Institute.

Ornstein, Norman et al. *1984. Vital Statistics on Congress, 1984–1985 Edition.* Washington, D.C.: American Enterprise Institute.

Ornstein, Norman. 1972. *Information, Resources and Legislative Decision-Making.* Unpublished Ph.D. dissertation, University of Michigan.

Parker, Glenn. 1980. "Sources of Change in Congressional District Attentiveness." *American Journal of Political Science* 24 (February):115–24.

———. and Roger H. Davidson. 1979. "Why Do Americans Love Their Congressman So Much More Than Their Congress?" *Legislative Studies Quarterly* 4 (February):53–61.

Perdue, Lewis. 1977. "The Million Dollar Advantage of Incumbency." *Washington Monthly* 9 (March):50–54.

Perry, James M. 1978. "Campaign Act: Congressmen Discover Computer and Use It to Keep Voters in Tow." *Wall Street Journal*, March 15:1, 33.

Peterson, Bill. 1983. "Senate's 1982 Mailing Costs Taxpayers More Than $48 Million." *Washington Post* February 19, 1983, p. a2.

Pincus, Walter. 1977a. "Hill Mailings Cost Millions, Stir Controversy." *Washington Post*, April 3:21.

———. 1977b. "Free Mail Helps Re-elect Congress." *Washington Post*, November 25, 1977, p. a1.

———. 1977c. "Plain Brown Wrappers From Congress." *Washington Post*, December 25:a4.

Pitkin, Hannah. 1967. *The Concept of Representation.* Berkeley, Calif.: University of California Press.

———. and Sara M. Shumer. 1982. "On Participation." *Democracy* 2 (Fall).

Porat, Marc. 1978. "Communications Policy in an Information Society." In *Communications for Tomorrow*, edited by Glen O. Robinson, pp. 3–60. New York: Praeger.

Powell, Lynda W. 1982. "Constituency Service and Electoral Margin in Congress." Paper presented at the 1982 meeting of the American Political Science Association.

Ranney, Austin. 1981. "The Working Conditions of Members of Parliament and Congress." In *The Role of the Legislature in Western Democracies*, edited by Norman Ornstein, pp. 67–76. Washington, D.C.: American Enterprise Institute.

Ridgeway, James. 1982. "The Men Who Stuff Your Mailbox." *Parade*, June 20, 1982, p. 15.

Robinson, Michael J. 1981. "Three faces of Congressional Media." In *The New Congress*, edited by Thomas Mann and Norman Ornstein, pp. 55–98. Washington, D.C.: American Enterprise Institute.

Rosenau, James N. 1974. *Citizenship Between Elections*. New York: The Free Press.

Rothman, Robert. 1983. "Congress Reluctant to Limit Member's Mailing Privileges." *Congressional Quarterly Weekly Report* 41 (July):1353–56.

Ryan, Frank. *Computing as an Aid to Political Effectiveness*. 1976. Hanover, N.H.: Dartmouth College Press.

Rundquist, Barry S. and Lyman Kellstedt. 1983 "Congressional Interaction with Constituents." Paper presented at the 1982 meeting of the American Political Science Association.

Saloma, John S. 1969. *Congress and the New Politics*. Boston: Little Brown.

Saperstein, Saundra. 1982. "The 'Ins' Have It." *Washington Post*, September 23, 1982, p. a1.

Shapiro, Joseph. 1982. "Why It's So Hard for Outs to Beat Ins," *U.S. News and World Report*, November 1:23.

Simon, Herbert. 1975. "The Consequence of Computers for Centralization and Decentralization," In *The Computer Age: A Twenty-Year View*, edited by Michael Dertouzous and Joel Moses. Cambridge, Mass.: MIT Press.

Skubik, Stephen, ed. 1968. *Handbook of Humor by Famous Politicians*. Washington, D.C.: Acropolis Books.

Staenberg, J. B. 1977. *The Use of Computers by House Members and the Staff for Official and Campaign Purposes: Legal and Ethical Issues*. Congressional Research Service Report no. 77-242 658/62 Washington, D.C.: Government Printing Office.

Staff Journal. 1982a. "If It's September, This Must Be the 'Lugar and Quayle Office'." *Congressional Staff Journal* (September/October):1–3.

———. 1982b. "Hope, Despair, Complexities, Delays Converge on Immigration Casework." *Congressional Staff Journal*, pp. 9–14.

———. 1982c. "Capitol Cases." *Congressional Staff Journal* (November/December):17–18.

Stolarek, John S., Robert M. Rood, Marcia Whicker Taylor. 1981. "Measuring Constituency Opinion in the U.S. House: Mail Versus Random Surveys." *Legislative Studies Quarterly* 6 (November):589–95.

Stone, Walter J. 1980. "The Dynamics of Constituency: Electoral Control in the House," *American Politics Quarterly* 8 (October):399–424.

Tacheron, Donald G. and Morris K. Udall. 1970. *The Job of the Congressman.* Indianapolis, Ind.: Bobbs-Merrill.

Udall, Morris K. 1964. "Legislative Questionnaire." *Congressional Record,* 88th Cong., 2nd Session, vol. 110, No. 17.
——. 1967. "The Right to Vote." *A Congressman's Report* 6 (January 20):1–3.
U.S., Congress, House. Commission on Administrative Review. 1977. *Final Report of the Commission on Administrative Review.* 95th Cong., 1st Session, House Document 95-272.
U.S., Congress, House. Committee on House Administration. 1980. *Congressional Handbook.* 96th Cong., 2nd Session.
U.S., Congress, Senate. Commission on the Operation of The Senate. 1977. *Senators: Office Ethics and Pressures.* 95th Cong., 1st Session.
U.S., Congress, Senate. Committee on Appropriations. Subcommittee on the Legislative Process. 1979. *Oversight on Computer Services in the Legislative Branch* (Hearing). 96th Cong., 1st Session.
U.S., Congress, Senate. Committee on Government Affairs. 1978. *Establishing Limitations on the Use of the Frank.* 95th Cong., 2nd Session. Report 95-566.
U.S., Congress, Senate. Committee on Rules and Administration. 1980 *Annual Report of the Technical Services Staff to the Chairman.* 96th Cong., 2nd Session, committee print.

Verba, Sidney and Richard Brody. 1970. "Participation, Policy Preferences and the War in Viet Nam." *Public Opinion Quarterly* 34 (Fall):325–32.
——. and Norman Nie. 1972 *Participation in America.* New York: Harper and Row.

Weissberg, Robert. 1979. "Assessing Legislator-constituency Policy Agreement." *Legislative Studies Quarterly* 4 (November):605–22.
Westin, T. Edward. 1973. "The Constituent Needs Help: Casework in the House of Representatives." In *To Be a Congressman,* edited by Sven Groennings and Jonathan Hawley, pp. 53–72. Washington, D.C.: Acropolis Books.
Wilcox, Walter. 1966. "The Congressional Poll and Non-poll." In *Public Opinion and Electoral Behavior,* edited by Edward C. Dreyer and Walter A. Rosenbaum, pp. 490–500. Belmont, Calif.: Wadsworth.
Wood, Fred B. 1979. *Video Conferencing via Satellite: Opening Congress to the People.* Washington, D.C.: George Washington University Press.
Wright, Jim. 1976. *You and Your Congressman.* New York: Capricorn Books.
Yadlosky, Elizabeth. 1981. *Franking Laws: Legal and Constitutional Issues.* Congressional Research Service Report no. 81-60s. Washington, D.C.: Government Printing Office.
——. 1982. Constitutionality of Financing Statute Upheld by U.S. District Court in *Common Cause v. Bolger.* Congressional Research Service Report No. 82-1555.

———. and Bonnie Bird. 1981. *Issues in the Franking Litigation.* Congressional Research Service Report no. 81-142s. Washington, D.C.: Government Printing Office.

———. and Jack Maskell. 1980. *The Congressional Frank: Statutory Provisions, Legislative History, Judicial Constructions and Some Proposals for Amending the Law,* Congressional Research Service Report no. 80-132d. Washington, D.C.: Government Printing Office.

Yiannakis, Diana E. 1979. "House Members' Communications Styles: Newsletters and Press Releases." Paper presented at the 1979 meeting of the Midwest Political Science Association.

———. 1981. "The Grateful Electorate: Casework and Congressional Elections." *American Journal of Political Science* 25 (August): 568–80. *Congressional Quarterly Weekly Report* 40 (September):2245–47.

INDEX

ABOUT THE AUTHOR

Stephen Frantzich is Associate Professor of Political Science at the U.S. Naval Academy. He received his Ph.D. from the University of Minnesota and specializes in the study of Congress and the impact of modern information technology on the political process. These interests merged with the publication of *Computers in Congress: The Politics of Information* (Beverly Hills: Sage Publications, 1982.) Studying the use of computers by Congress involved an in-depth analysis of congressional-constituent communications and spawned this book. Dr. Frantzich serves as a consultant to a wide variety of academic and campaign and research organizations.